William Howard Doane

Songs of the Kingdom

Prepared for the Use of Young People's Societies...

William Howard Doane

Songs of the Kingdom
Prepared for the Use of Young People's Societies...

ISBN/EAN: 9783337172084

Printed in Europe, USA, Canada, Australia, Japan

Cover: Foto ©Thomas Meinert / pixelio.de

More available books at **www.hansebooks.com**

Songs of the Kingdom

PREPARED FOR THE USE OF

YOUNG PEOPLE'S SOCIETIES

AND ADAPTED FOR

PRAYER MEETINGS, SUNDAY SCHOOLS AND THE HOME.

BY

W. HOWARD DOANE.

PHILADELPHIA:
AMERICAN BAPTIST PUBLICATION SOCIETY
1420 Chestnut Street.

Copyright, 1896, by W. H. Doane.

PREFATORY NOTES.

The Editor has earnestly sought in the selection and adaptation of the Music and Hymns in "Songs of the Kingdom," to give a place to such as seemed to him best to voice the praises, pleadings, and aspirations of Christian hearts in the worship of the Lord Jesus Christ.

Special acknowledgments are due to Rev. Robert Lowry, D. D., for his valuable contributions and assistance, also to The Biglow & Main Co., New York, and others, for permission to use copyright music.

W. H. DOANE.

The Committee of the Baptist Young People's Union of America, appointed to have general charge of the preparation of the Song-book, are gratified to present "Songs of the Kingdom" to the public. The primary purpose of the book is to supply an attractive collection of hymns and tunes for the use of Baptist Young People in their devotional meetings and in their rallies and conventions; also a popular song book for general use in Sunday Schools, Prayer Meetings, and in the Home. As a preliminary step a general request was made for lists of hymns suitable for use in such a collection. Replies were received from hundreds of pastors and active workers in all parts of the United States and Canada. The grand old hymns of the Church, the songs that have won immortality, were numerously represented in the lists, confirming the committee in their conviction that the book should contain a goodly representation of these tried and tested favorites; songs that represented the best evangelical sentiment were, by common consent, expected to have a large place in the book.

Appreciating the fact that after carefully winnowing the old favorites, new music must be added to make the book complete, we counted ourselves fortunate in being able to secure the services of W. Howard Doane, Mus. Doc., to whom was entrusted the musical editorship of the entire work. He has rendered invaluable service. His well known musical talent is apparent throughout the book.

With this brief prefatory statement, "Songs of the Kingdom" is introduced to the public. More than fifty authors are represented in its pages. We congratulate the Baptist Young People on having a song book of their own, and pray that the Lord may bless its use to the good of the young in life and the young in heart throughout our Baptist Zion.

F. L. WILKINS, Ch'n.
IRA M. PRICE, Sec'y.
P. S. HENSON,
L. A. CRANDALL,
JESSE A. BALDWIN,

Song Book Com., B. Y. P. U. A.

SONGS OF THE KINGDOM.

1. More Like Jesus.

"We shall be like him." —1 John 3: 2.

Fanny J. Crosby.   W. H. Doane.

Slow, with feeling.

Copyright, 1869, by W. H. Doane.

1. More like Je-sus would I be; Let my Saviour dwell with me—
2. If He hears the ra-ven's cry, If His ev-er-watch-ful eye
3. More like Je-sus when I pray, More like Je-sus day by day,

Fill my soul with peace and love—Make me gen-tle as a dove;
Marks the sparrows when they fall, Sure-ly He will hear my call;
May I rest me by His side, Where the tranquil wa-ters glide;

More like Je-sus, while I go, Pil-grim in this world be-low;
He will teach me how to live, All my sim-ple tho'ts for-give;
Born of Him, thro' grace renewed, By His love my will subdued,

Poor in spir-it would I be— Let my Saviour dwell in me.
Pure in heart I still would be— Let my Saviour dwell in me.
Rich in faith I still would be— Let my Saviour dwell in me.

(3)

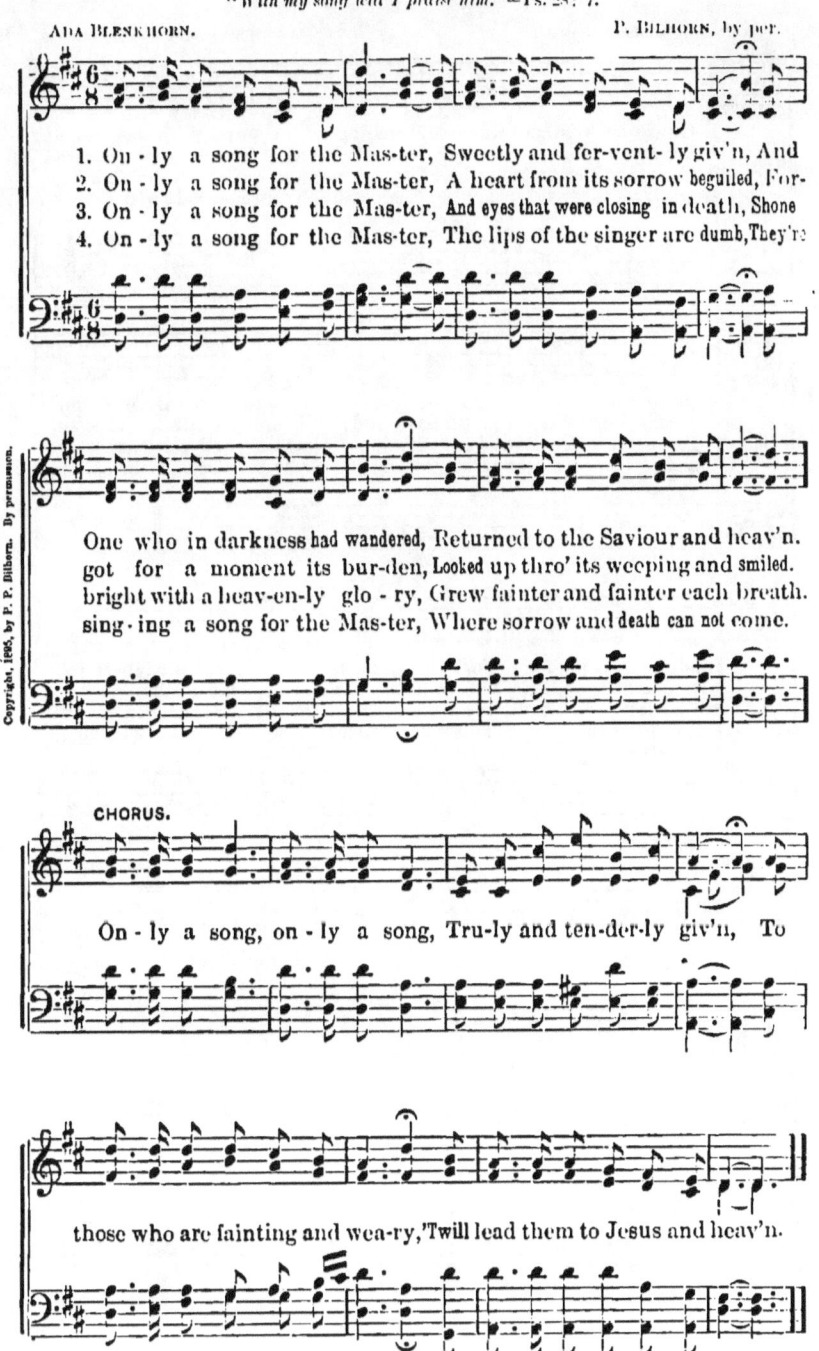

Choose Ye This Day.

"Choose you this day whom ye will serve."—JOSH. 24: 15.

REV. S. S. CRYOR, D. D.
P. P. BILHORN, by per.

1. Sin-ner, choose to-day your Saviour, By whose blood your soul was bought;
2. Without Christ your life is wast-ed, All its rich-es are but dross;
3. Oh, far bet-ter you had nev-er Seen the light of earthly day,
4. Choose while others then are waiting For the choice that you may make;

Time is fleet-ing, hope is cheating, Do not spend your life for naught.
If you still re-fuse His mer-cy, You must suf-fer endless loss.
Than to hear the Spir-it call-ing, While you turn unmoved away.
And while souls are now de-bat-ing, Take the cross for Je-sus' sake.

copyright, 1895, by P. P. Bilhorn. By permission.

List-en to God's voice entreating, Harden not your heart to-day;

Let not Sa-tan's acts de-ceiv-ing, Tempt you longer to de-lay

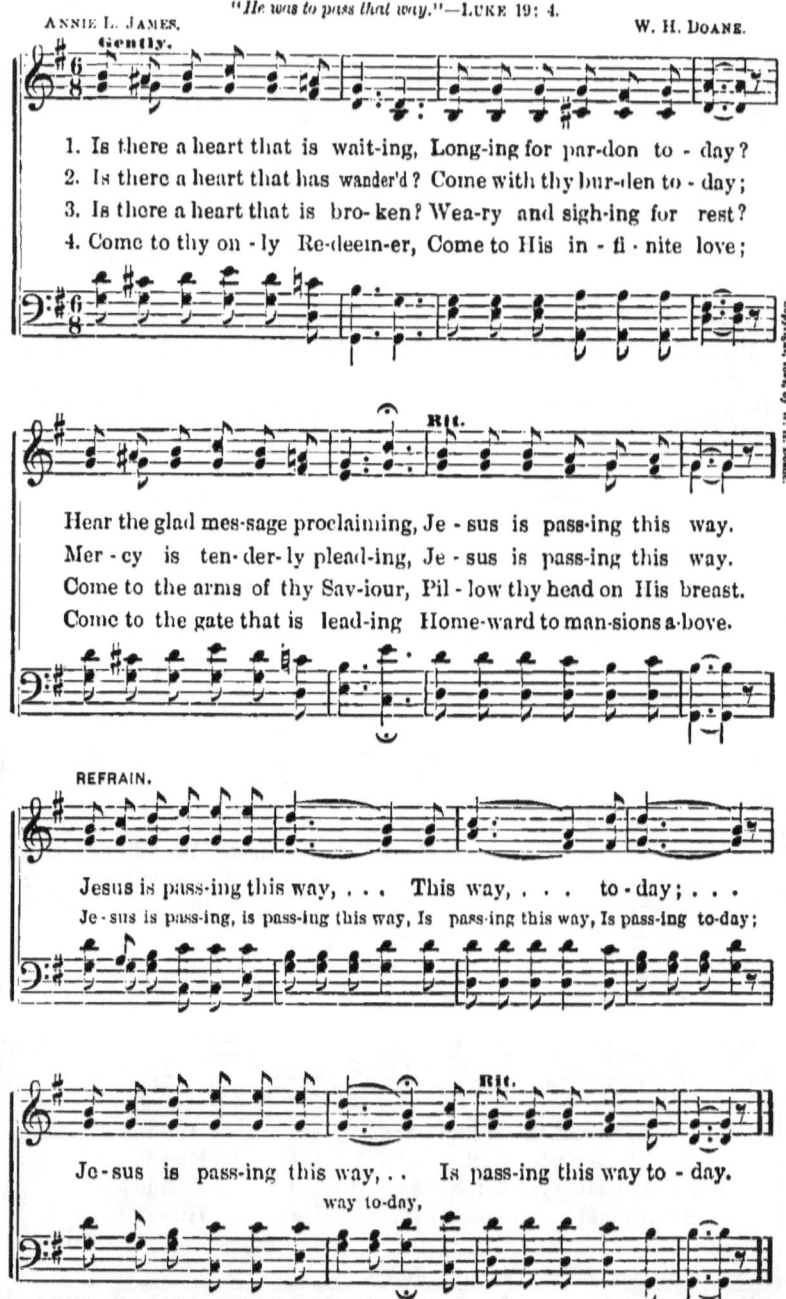

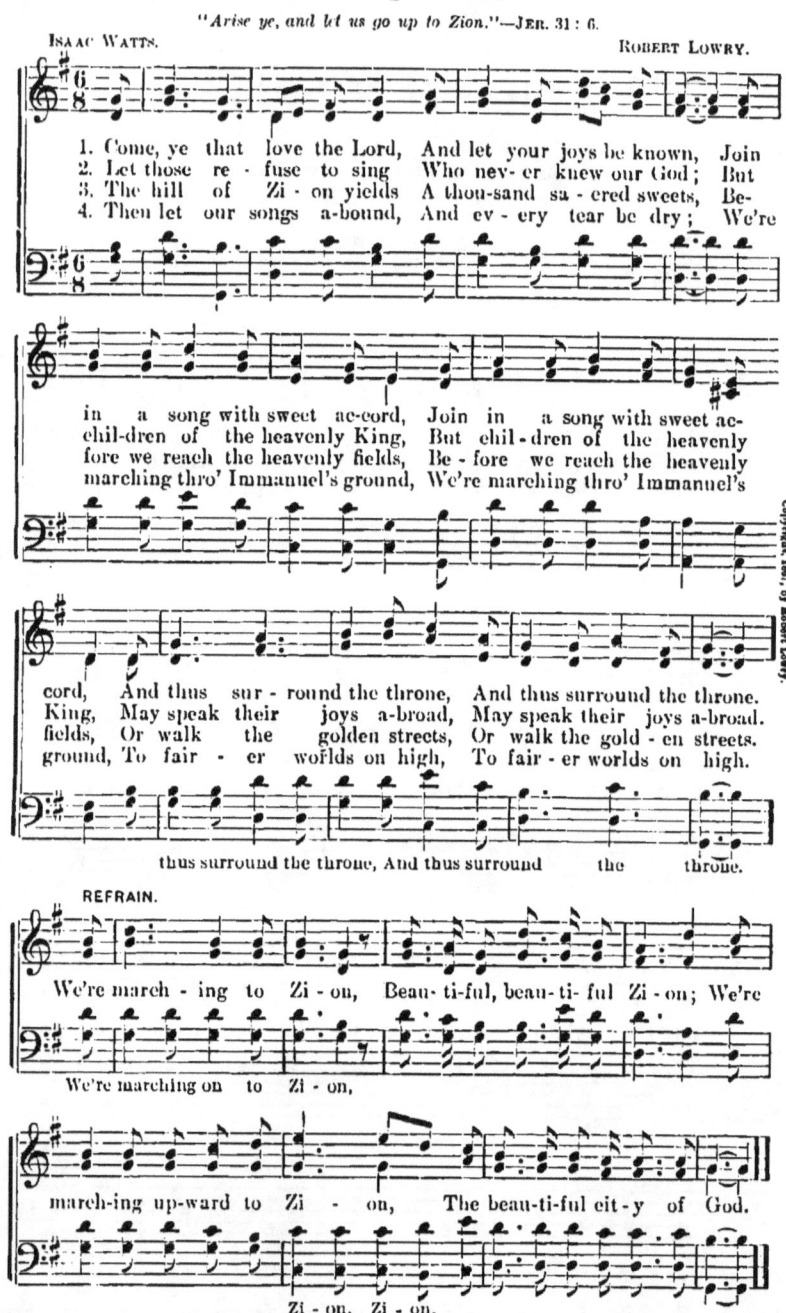

19. Seeking for Me.

"I will both search My sheep, and seek them out." — EZEK. 34: 11.

A. N.
E. E. HASTY, by per.

1. Je-sus, my Saviour, to Beth-le-hem came, Born in a man-ger to sor-row and shame; Oh, it was won-der-ful, blest be His name! Seeking for me, for me!
2. Je-sus, my Saviour, on Cal-va-ry's tree, Paid the great debt, and my soul He set free; Oh, it was won-der-ful, how could it be? Dy-ing for me, for me!
3. Je-sus, my Saviour, the same as of old, While I was wand'ring a-far from the fold; Gently and long did He plead with my soul, Calling for me, for me!
4. Je-sus, my Saviour, will come from on high—Sweet is the promise as wea-ry years fly; Oh, I shall see Him de-scend-ing the sky, Com-ing for me, for me!

REFRAIN.

For me! . . . . for me! . . . .
Seek-ing for me! Seek-ing for me! Seek-ing for me! Seek-ing for me!
Dy-ing for me! Dy-ing for me! Dy-ing for me! Dy-ing for me!
Call-ing for me! Call-ing for me! Call-ing for me! Call-ing for me!
Com-ing for me! Com-ing for me! Com-ing for me! Com-ing for me!

Oh, it was won-der-ful—blest be His name! Seek-ing for me, for me!
Oh, it was won-der-ful—how could it be? Dy-ing for me, for me!
Gen-tly and long did He plead with my soul, Call-ing for me, for me!
Oh, I shall see Him de-scend-ing the sky, Com-ing for me, for me!

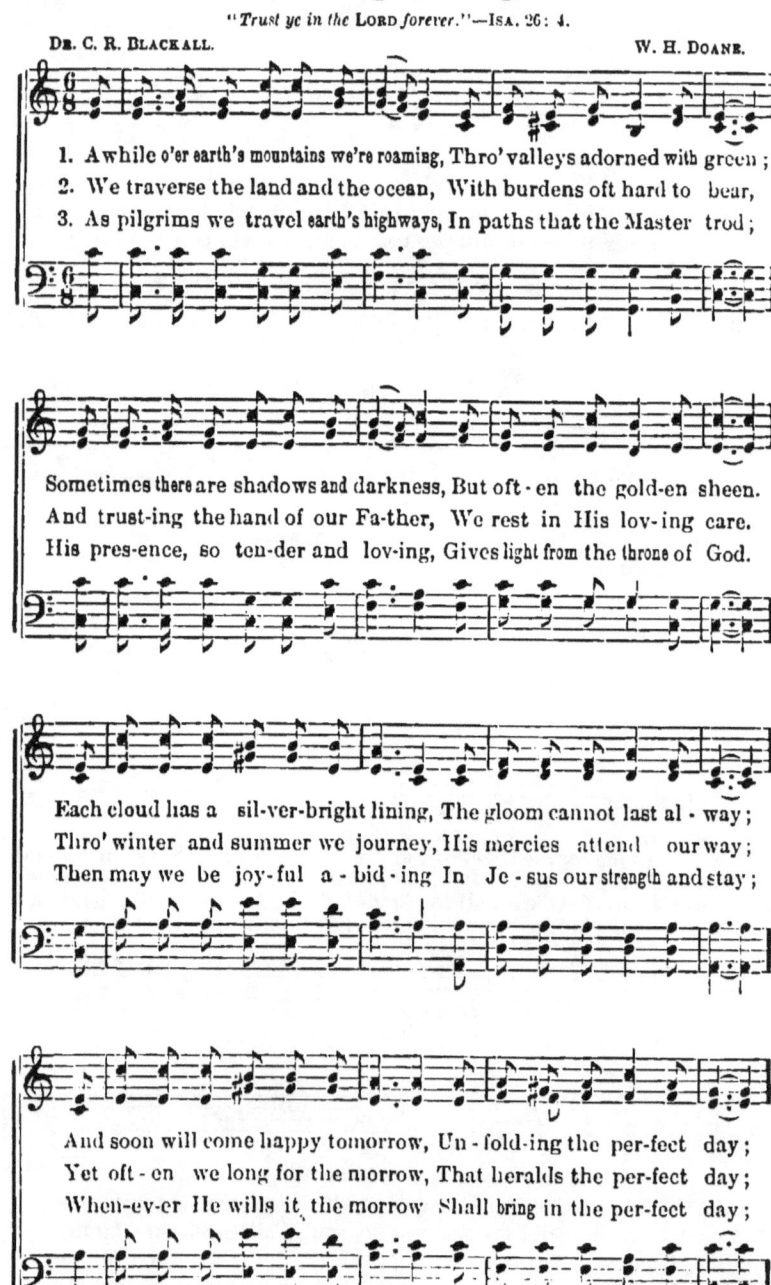

23. Lord, Where Thou Wilt.

"The perfect will of God." Rom. 12: 2.

1. Lord, where Thou wilt—it matters not to me, If Thou art near, and I can cling to Thee; For I am weak, so weak, I am a-fraid To take one step with-out Thy kindly aid.
2. Lord, where Thou wilt—it matters not to me, Tho' skies may frown, and dark my path may be; I am con-tent, since Thou, my Life, my Light, Canst pierce the veil that hangs o'er darkest night.
3. Lord, where Thou wilt—it matters not to me, If faith's clear eye the po-lar star may see; If I can read my ti-tle to a home Where sin and death and night can nev-er come.

REFRAIN.
Lead Thou my way, my fainting heart sus-tain; Lead Thou my way, and make my du-ty plain; Lead Thou my way, Then shall I fear no ill, If Thou, my "Rod and Staff," art with me still.

Christ, My Rock.

"The rock of my salvation." — Ps. 89: 26.

BERTHA J. MASON.   W. H. DOANE.

Copyright, 1894, by W. H. Doane.

1. I will sing of my sal-va-tion, Christ, my Rock; On the on-ly sure foun-da-tion, Christ, my Rock; I have built my house for-ev-er, Where the flood can reach me nev-er, Bless-ed Hope of my sal-va-tion, Christ, my Rock.

2. I will praise the pow'r that holds me, Christ, my Rock; I will sing the love that folds me, Christ, my Rock; Sol-id Rock unmoved, a-bid-ing, While e-ter-nal years are glid-ing, Bless-ed Hope of my sal-va-tion, Christ, my Rock.

3. On the towering heights re-pos-ing, Christ, my Rock; When these eyes on earth are clos-ing, Christ, my Rock; Then my soul shall waft the sto-ry, Thro' the gates of end-less glo-ry, Bless-ed Hope of my sal-va-tion, Christ, my Rock.

28. From the Cross.

"Nailing it to his cross."—COL. 2: 14.

ROGER H. LYON. ROBERT LOWRY.

1. I walk re-joic-ing from the cross, With Christ, my ris-en Lord, In hope of His e-ter-nal life, And by His ho-ly word. From the cross, from the cross, With Christ, my ris-en Lord.
2. Oh, peace! oh, comfort! from the cross The light of glo-ry streams; Makes clear the way thro' death's dark vale, And leads me by its beams. From the cross, from the cross, The light of glo-ry streams.
3. Oh, joy! oh, rapture! thro' the cross, Death's port-al fall-en lies; And, lo, my coming Lord appears, To bear me to the skies. Thro' the cross, thro' the cross, Death's port-al fall-en lies.
4. O sin-ner, standing at the cross, He bids you look and live; Yield up your heart with all its dross, That He may pardon give. At the cross, at the cross, He bids you look and live.

Copyright, 1890, by Robert Lowry.

29. Happy Day.

"Whoso trusteth in the Lord, happy is he."—PROV. 16: 20.

PHILIP DODDRIDGE, D.D. E. F. RIMBAULT.

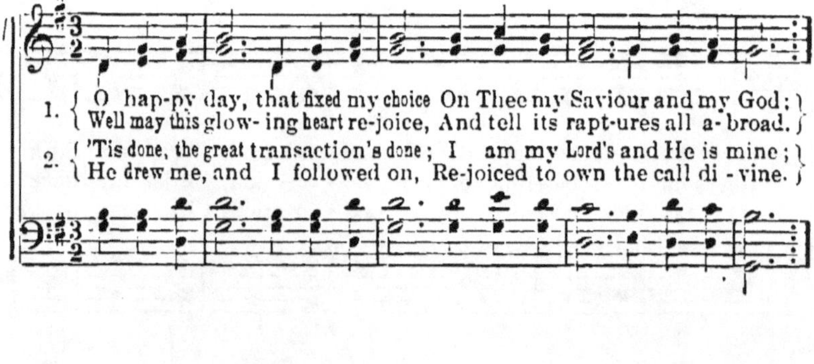

1. { O hap-py day, that fixed my choice On Thee my Saviour and my God; }
   { Well may this glow-ing heart re-joice, And tell its rapt-ures all a-broad. }
2. { 'Tis done, the great transaction's done; I am my Lord's and He is mine; }
   { He drew me, and I followed on, Re-joiced to own the call di-vine. }

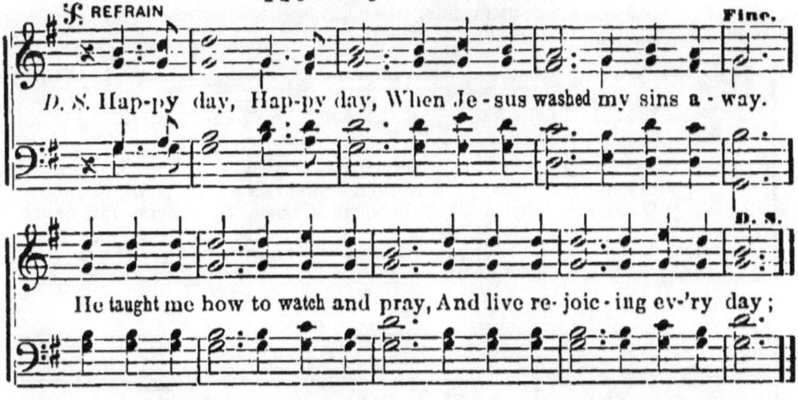

Happy Day. Concluded.

D. S. Hap-py day, Hap-py day, When Je-sus washed my sins a-way.

He taught me how to watch and pray, And live re-joic-ing ev-'ry day;

3 Now rest, my long-divided heart,
Fixed on this blissful center, rest;
Here have I found a nobler part,
Here heavenly pleasures fill my breast.

4 High heaven that hears the solemn vow,
That vow renewed shall daily hear,
Till in life's latest hour I bow,
And bless in death a bond so dear.

30 Lead Me, I Pray.

"Lead me."—Ps. 31:3.

FANNY J. CROSBY.   W. H. DOANE.

1. Sav-iour, Thy name I plead, Weak as a bruis-ed reed, Grant me the
2. Sav-iour and Friend di-vine, All that I have is Thine, Keep Thou this
3. Sav-iour who died for me, Hide Thou my life in Thee, Where'er my
4. Grant Thou my earnest pray'r, Safe thro' this world of care, Home to thy

grace I need, Lead me, I pray.
heart of mine, Lead me, I pray.
path may be, Lead me, I pray.
man-sions fair, Lead me, I pray.

REFRAIN.

Lead me, I pray, Lead me to-day, Lead me, lead me, Lead me, I pray.

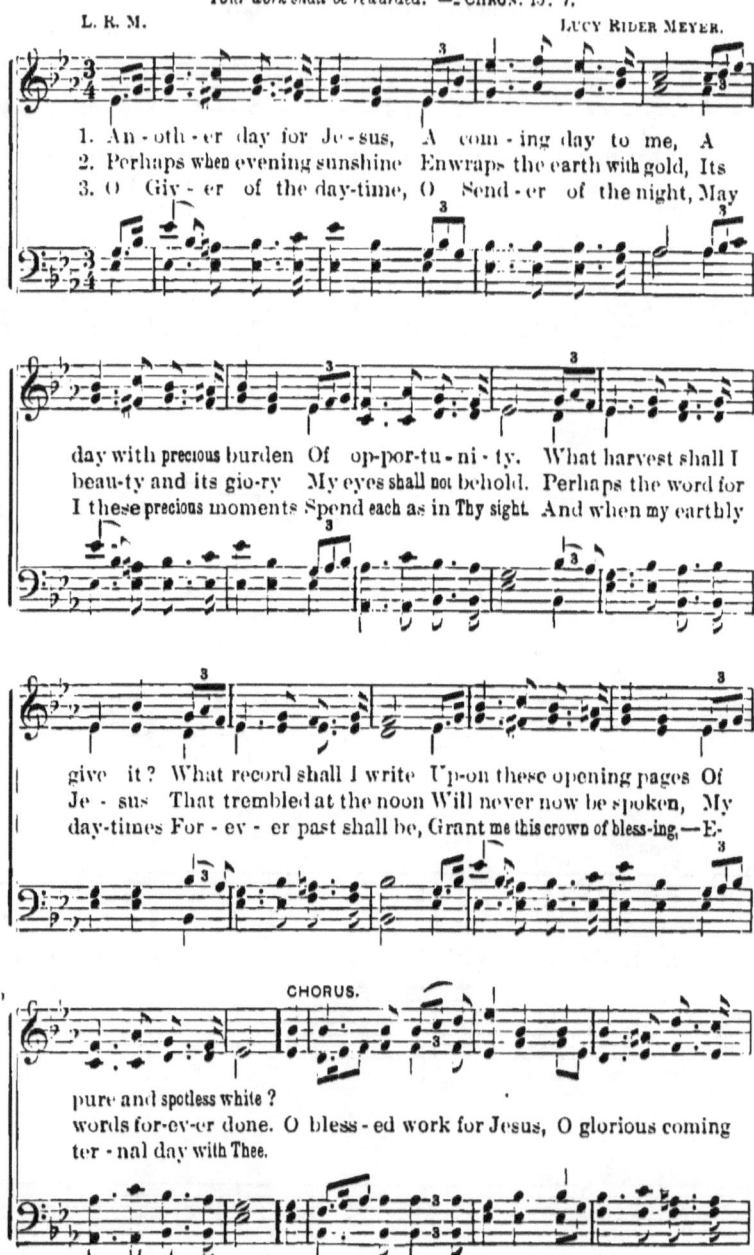

Another Day for Jesus. Concluded.

day, Thy golden hours may lad-en be With work for Him who died for me; O bless-ed work for Je - sus, O glo-rious coming day.

34. I'll Live for Him.

"*To me to live is Christ.*"—Phil. 1: 21.

C. R. Dunbar.

1. My life, my love I give to Thee, Thou Lamb of God, who died for me;
2. I now believe Thou dost receive, For Thou hast died that I may live;
3. O Thou, who died on Cal-va-ry, To save my soul and make me free,

Cho. *I'll live for Him who died for me, How hap-py then my life shall be;*

O may I ev - er faith-ful be, My Saviour and my God!
And now henceforth I'll trust in Thee, My Saviour and my God!
I con - se-crate my life to Thee, My Saviour and my God!

I'll live for Him who died for me, My Sav-iour and my God!

38. Holy, Holy! Lord God Almighty!

"They rest not day nor night, saying, Holy, Holy, Holy, Lord God Almighty, which was, and is, and is to come." — REV. 4: 8.

REGINALD HEBER, D. D.   REV. J. B. DYKES.

1. Ho-ly, ho-ly, ho-ly! Lord God Al-might-y! Ear-ly in the morn-ing our song shall rise to Thee; Ho-ly, ho-ly, ho-ly! Mer-ci-ful and Mighty, God in three per-sons, bless-ed Trin-i-ty!
2. Ho-ly, ho-ly, ho-ly! all the saints a-dore Thee, Cast-ing down their gold-en crowns a-round the glass-y sea; Cher-u-bim and ser-a-phim falling down be-fore Thee, Which wert, and art, and ev-er-more shalt be.
3. Ho-ly, ho-ly, ho-ly! tho' the dark-ness hide Thee, Tho' the eye of sin-ful man Thy glo-ry may not see; On-ly Thou art ho-ly, there is none be-side Thee, Per-fect in pow'r, in love, and pu-ri-ty.
4. Ho-ly, ho-ly, ho-ly! Lord God Al-might-y! All Thy works shall praise Thy name in earth, and sky, and sea; Ho-ly, ho-ly, ho-ly! Mer-ci-ful and Might-y, God in three per-sons, bless-ed Trin-i-ty! A-men.

39. The Grace of Our Lord Jesus Christ.

"The grace of our Lord Jesus Christ." — ROM. 16: 24.

W. F. SHERWIN.

The grace of our Lord Je-sus Christ be with you all. A-men.

40. There's a Place for Me.

"And yet there is room." —LUKE 14: 22.

E. E. HEWITT.   WM. J. KIRKPATRICK.

1. There's a place for me at the Saviour's cross, When in sorrow bending low;
2. There's a place for me at the Mer-cy seat, When in Je-sus' name I plead,
3. There's a place for me in His harvest field, And a work for me to do;
4. There's a place for me in the Father's house, There are mansions bright and fair;

There is cleansing pow'r in the precious blood, There's salvation in its flow.
When I lift my eyes to the throne above, Where He lives to in-ter-cede.
If I love the Lord who redeemed my soul, Let me serve Him tru-ly, too.
With my robes made white thro' His saving blood, There's a crown for me to wear.

CHORUS.

There's a place for me, blessed place for me, At the cross where my Saviour died;

There's a place for me in His lov-ing breast, Ever there may I a-bide.

Copyright, 1889, by Wm. J. Kirkpatrick.

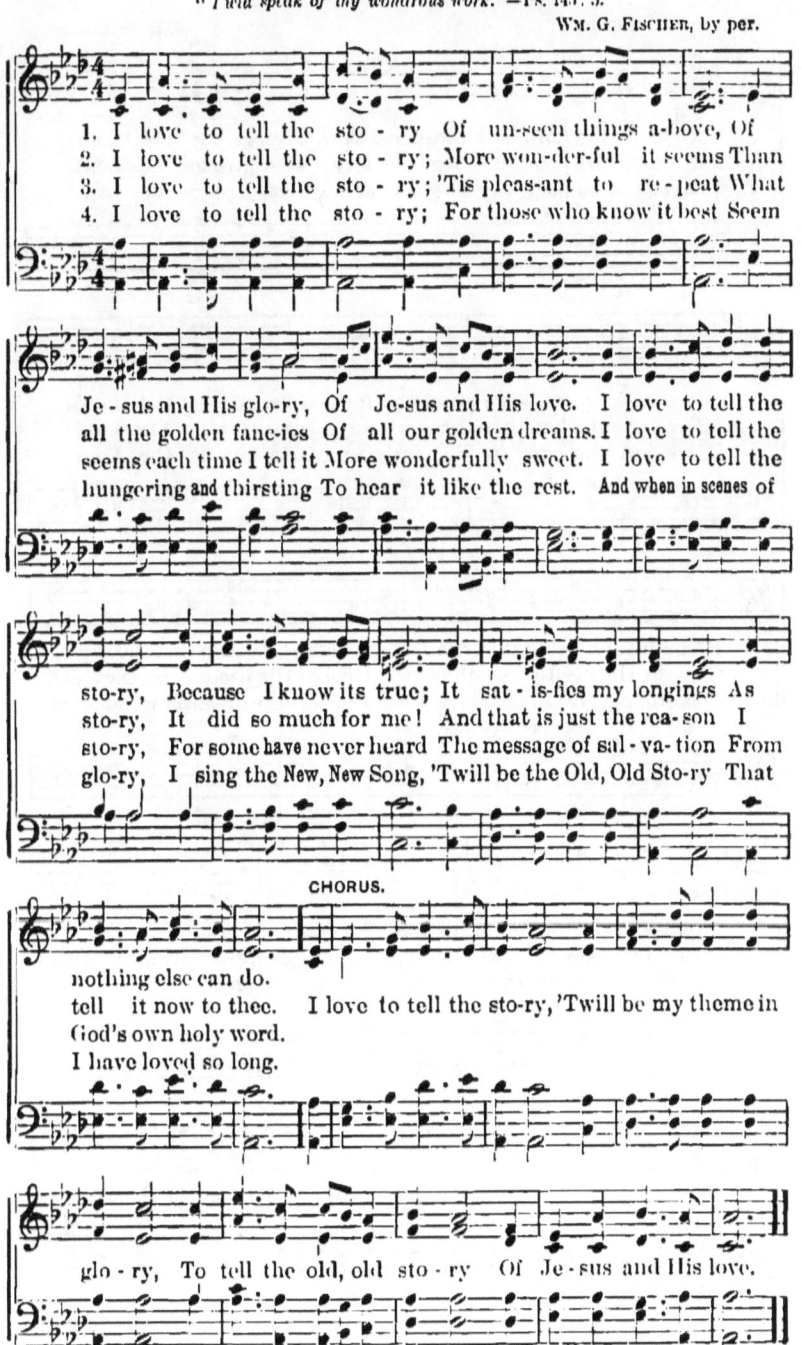

42. Give as the Lord hath Prospered Thee.

"God loveth a cheerful giver." — 2 Cor. 9: 7.

PALMER HARTSOUGH. J. H. FILLMORE.

1. Give as the Lord hath prospered thee, Give, give to the Lord;
2. Give to the poor a-long the way, Give, give to the Lord;
3. Give, tho' so poor thy gift may seem, Give, give to the Lord;

Give with a will-ing mind and free, Give, give to the Lord;
Give to the hea-then far a-way, Give, give to the Lord;
Give but the cup in Je-sus' name, Give, give to the Lord;

He hath supplied thee o'er and o'er, Blessed thee in basket and in store,
Give to His need-y as they cry, Give to His peo-ple ere they die,
Cheerful then give the good thou hast, Fearless thy bread on waters cast,

Promised to fill thee more and more, Thy gracious Lord.
Give to His gos-pel that it fly,
It will re-turn to thee at last In harvests great.

REFRAIN.
Oh, give, give, give. Give, give with a willing hand, Give, give, with a liberal hand, Give (give) at His blest command,

Copyright 1896, by Fillmore Bros.

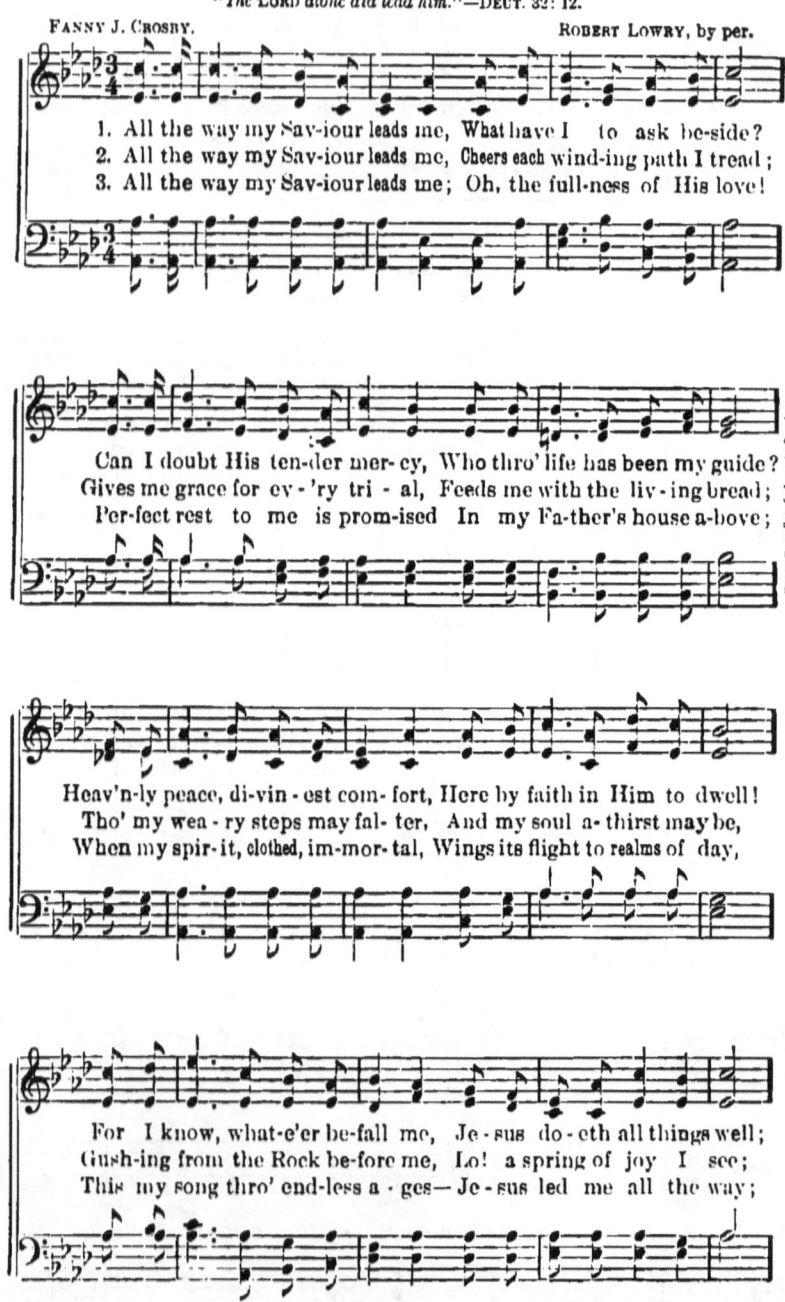

All the Way. Concluded.

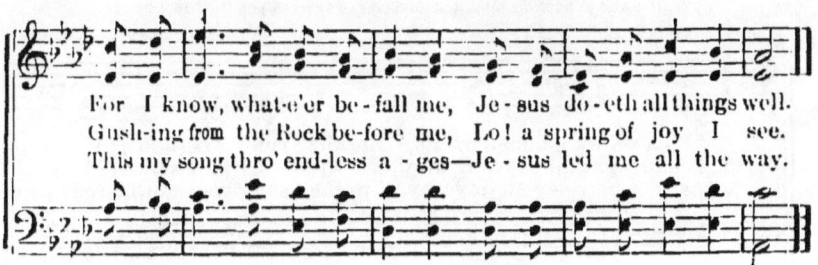

For I know, what-e'er be-fall me, Je-sus do-eth all things well.
Gush-ing from the Rock be-fore me, Lo! a spring of joy I see.
This my song thro' end-less a-ges—Je-sus led me all the way.

45 Lead, Kindly Light.

"Send out thy light and thy truth: let them lead me."—Ps. 43: 3.

JOHN H. NEWMAN.　　　　　　　　　　　　JOHN B. DYKES.

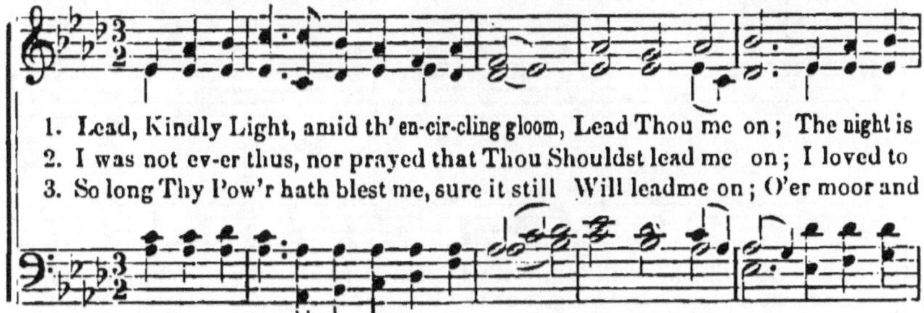

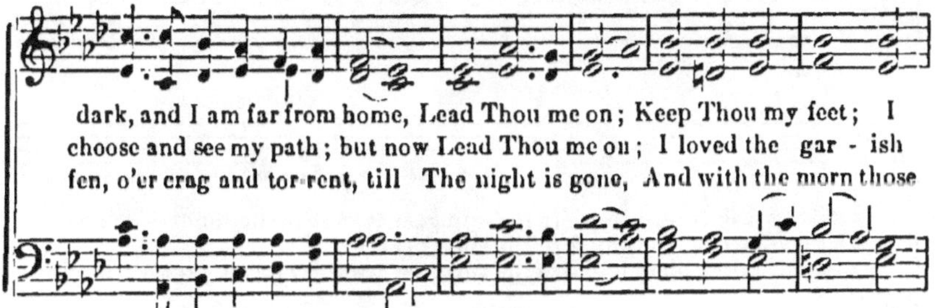

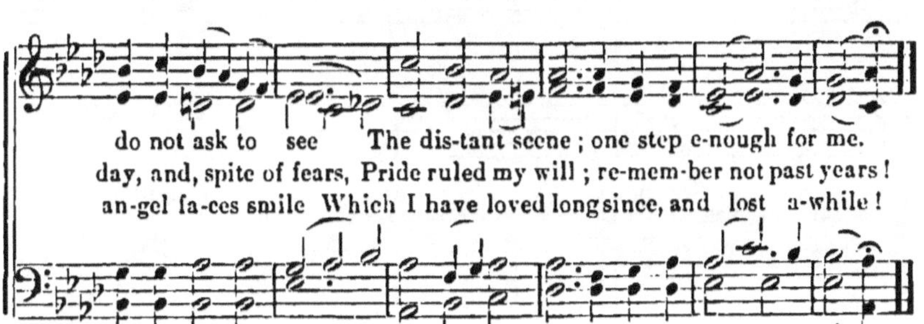

1. Lead, Kindly Light, amid th' en-cir-cling gloom, Lead Thou me on; The night is
dark, and I am far from home, Lead Thou me on; Keep Thou my feet; I
do not ask to see The dis-tant scene; one step e-nough for me.

2. I was not ev-er thus, nor prayed that Thou Shouldst lead me on; I loved to
choose and see my path; but now Lead Thou me on; I loved the gar-ish
day, and, spite of fears, Pride ruled my will; re-mem-ber not past years!

3. So long Thy Pow'r hath blest me, sure it still Will lead me on; O'er moor and
fen, o'er crag and tor-rent, till The night is gone, And with the morn those
an-gel fa-ces smile Which I have loved long since, and lost a-while!

46. Ere the Sun goes Down.

"Walk while ye have the light, lest darkness come upon you."—JOHN 12: 17.

JOSEPHINE POLLARD.　　　　　　　　　　　　　　　E. S. LORENZ. By per.

1. I have work e-nough to do, Ere the sun goes down; For myself and kin-dred too, Ere the sun goes down; Ev - 'ry
i - dle whis-per still-ing, With a pur-pose firm and will-ing, All my
dai - ly task ful-fill-ing, Ere the sun goes down. Ere the sun goes
down, Ere the sun goes down; For the night is fast de-

2. I must speak the lov-ing word, Ere the sun goes down; I must
let my voice be heard, Ere the sun goes down; Ev - 'ry
cry of pit - y heed-ing, For the in-jured in - ter-ced-ing, To the
light the lost ones lead-ing, Ere the sun goes down.

3. As I jour-ney on my way, Ere the sun goes down, God's com-
mands I must o - bey, Ere the sun goes down; There are
sins that need con-fess-ing, There are wrongs that need re-dress-ing, If I
would ob-tain a bless-ing, Ere the sun goes down. Ere the sun goes down, Ere the
sun goes down, Ere the sun goes down, Ere the sun goes down;

CHORUS.

Ere the Sun goes Down. Concluded.

scend-ing, And my life will have an end-ing, When the sun goes down.
When the sun

47. The Christian Hero.

"Quit you like men." —1 Cor. 16: 23.

W. H. NEVINS. Arr.

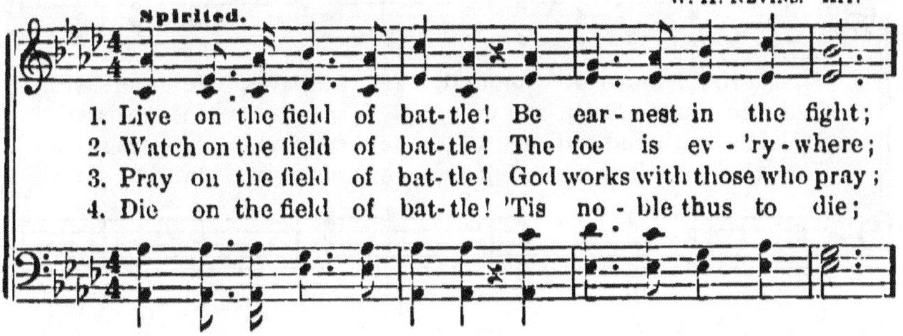

Spirited.

1. Live on the field of bat-tle! Be ear-nest in the fight;
2. Watch on the field of bat-tle! The foe is ev-'ry-where;
3. Pray on the field of bat-tle! God works with those who pray;
4. Die on the field of bat-tle! 'Tis no-ble thus to die;

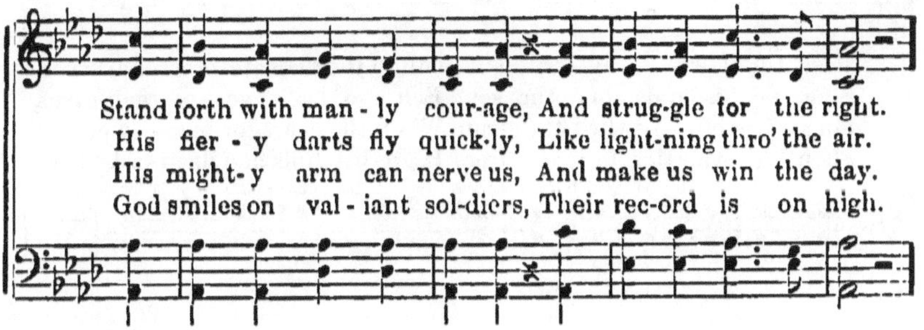

Stand forth with man-ly cour-age, And strug-gle for the right.
His fier-y darts fly quick-ly, Like light-ning thro' the air.
His might-y arm can nerve us, And make us win the day.
God smiles on val-iant sol-diers, Their rec-ord is on high.

Live! live! live! live! On the field of bat-tle.
Watch! watch! watch! watch! On the field of bat-tle.
Pray! pray! pray! pray! On the field of bat-tle.
Die! die! die! die! On the field of bat-tle.

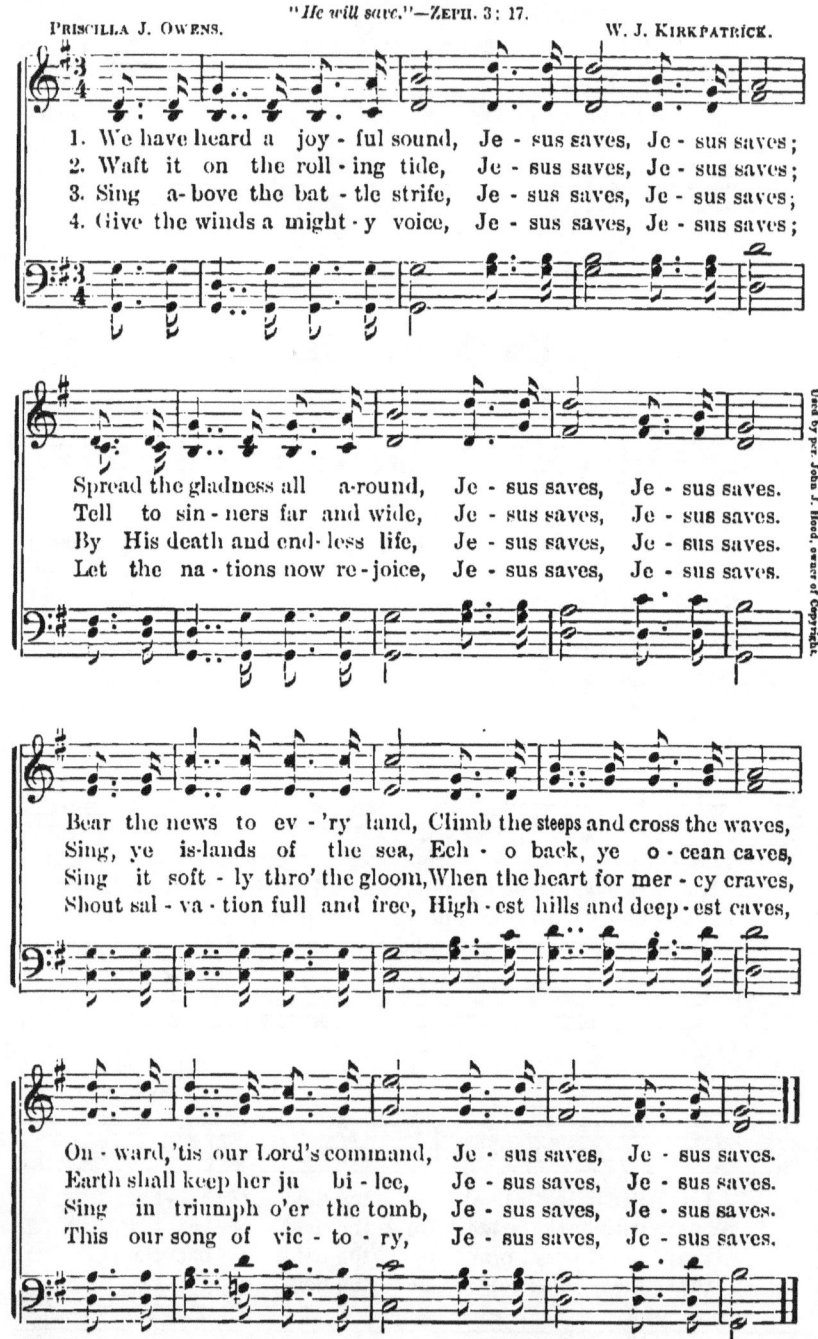

49. There's a Promise from the Lord.

"And this is the promise . . . eternal life." —1 JOHN 2 : 25.

FANNY J. CROSBY.   W. H. DOANE.

1. There's a promise from the Lord, Hal-le-lu-jah! 'Tis re-cord-ed in his word, Hal-le-lu-jah! That the faithful He'll re-ward, Hal-le-lu-jah! And that promise I be-lieve, Praise His name.
2. Oh, my heart is full of song, Hal-le-lu-jah! I am sing-ing all day long, Hal-le-lu-jah! In my weakness I am strong, Hal-le-lu-jah! For my strength is in the Lord, Praise His name.
3. Oh, His wondrous grace to me, Hal-le-lu-jah! Shall my theme for-ev-er be, Hal-le-lu-jah! With His blood He made me free, Hal-le-lu-jah! I am hap-py in His love, Praise His name.
4. To the pal-ace gates on high, Hal-le-lu-jah! He will guide me with his eye, Hal-le-lu-jah! I shall see Him by and by, Hal-le-lu-jah! And in glo-ry at His feet, Praise His name;

CHORUS.

Hal-le-lu-jah! Hal-le-lu-jah! I am trusting in the Lord, Halle-lu-jah! Hal-le-lu-jah! Hal-le-lu-jah! I am trusting in the Lord, Praise His name.

Copyright, 1896, by W. H. Doane.

52. Nearer, My God.

"Draw near with a true heart." — HEB. 10: 22.

SARAH F. ADAMS. DR. LOWELL MASON. By per.

1. Nearer, my God, to Thee,—Nearer to Thee! E'en tho' it be a cross That raiseth me; Still all my song shall be, Nearer, my God, to Thee, Nearer to Thee.

2 Though like the wanderer,
The sun gone down,
Darkness comes over me,
My rest a stone,
Yet in my dreams I'd be
Nearer, my God, to Thee,
Nearer to Thee!

3 There let my way appear
Steps unto heaven;
All that Thou sendest me
In mercy given;
Angels to beckon me
Nearer, my God, to Thee,
Nearer to Thee!

53. More Love to Thee.

"Continue ye in my love." — JOHN 15: 9.

MRS. E. P. PRENTISS. W. H. DOANE.

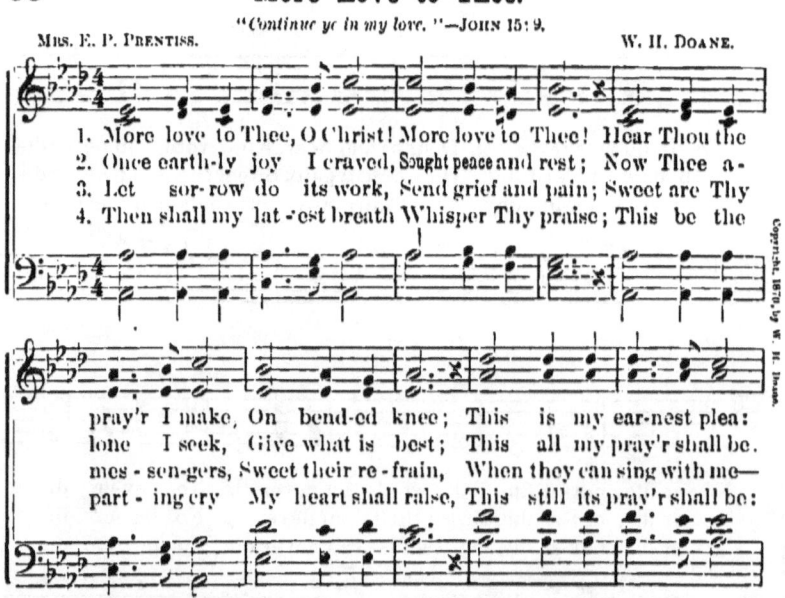

1. More love to Thee, O Christ! More love to Thee! Hear Thou the pray'r I make, On bended knee; This is my earnest plea:
2. Once earthly joy I craved, Sought peace and rest; Now Thee alone I seek, Give what is best; This all my pray'r shall be.
3. Let sorrow do its work, Send grief and pain; Sweet are Thy messengers, Sweet their refrain, When they can sing with me—
4. Then shall my latest breath Whisper Thy praise; This be the parting cry My heart shall raise, This still its pray'r shall be:

Copyright, 1870, by W. H. Doane.

More Love to Thee. Concluded.

More love, O Christ, to Thee, More love to Thee, More love to Thee.

54
I Need Thee Every Hour.

"God shall supply all your need."—PHIL. 4: 19.

MRS. ANNIE S. HAWKS.   ROBERT LOWRY.

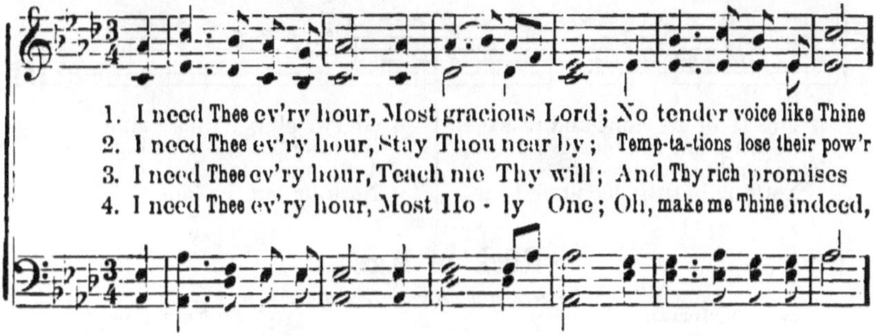

1. I need Thee ev'ry hour, Most gracious Lord; No tender voice like Thine
2. I need Thee ev'ry hour, Stay Thou near by; Temp-ta-tions lose their pow'r
3. I need Thee ev'ry hour, Teach me Thy will; And Thy rich promises
4. I need Thee ev'ry hour, Most Ho - ly One; Oh, make me Thine indeed,

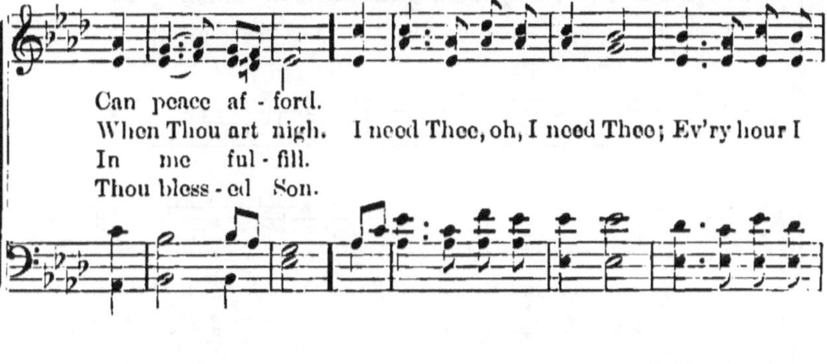

REFRAIN.

Can peace af - ford.
When Thou art nigh.   I need Thee, oh, I need Thee; Ev'ry hour I
In me ful - fill.
Thou bless - ed Son.

need Thee; Oh, bless me now, my Sav-iour, I come to Thee.

Copyright, 1872, by Robert Lowry.

55. Nothing but the Blood.

"Without shedding of blood is no remission." — HEB. 9: 22.

R. L.
ROBERT LOWRY.

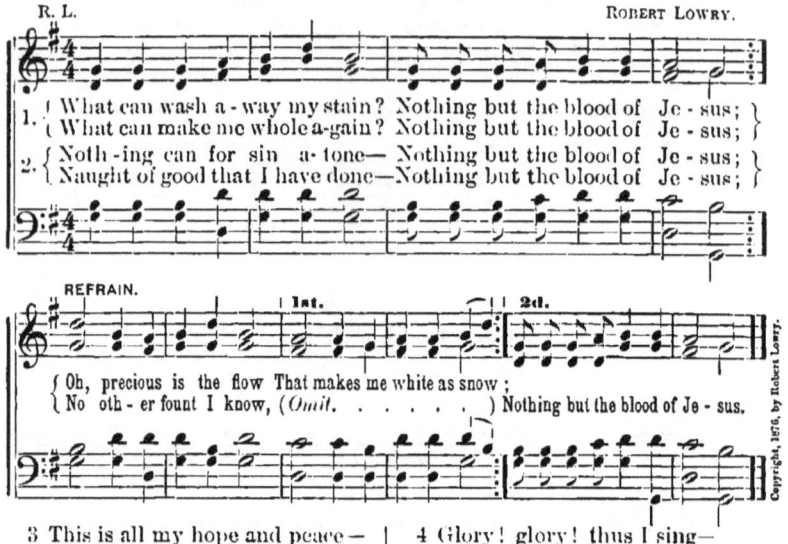

1. What can wash a-way my stain? Nothing but the blood of Je-sus;
   What can make me whole a-gain? Nothing but the blood of Je-sus;
2. Nothing can for sin a-tone— Nothing but the blood of Je-sus;
   Naught of good that I have done— Nothing but the blood of Je-sus;

REFRAIN.

Oh, precious is the flow That makes me white as snow;
No other fount I know, (*Omit* . . . . .) Nothing but the blood of Je-sus.

Copyright, 1876, by Robert Lowry.

3 This is all my hope and peace—
  Nothing but the blood of Jesus;
  This is all my righteousness—
  Nothing but the blood of Jesus.

4 Glory! glory! thus I sing—
  Nothing but the blood of Jesus;
  All my praise for this I bring—
  Nothing but the blood of Jesus.

56. Rock of Ages.

"The rock of my refuge." — Ps. 94: 22.

REV. A. M. TOPLADY.
DR. THOS. HASTINGS.

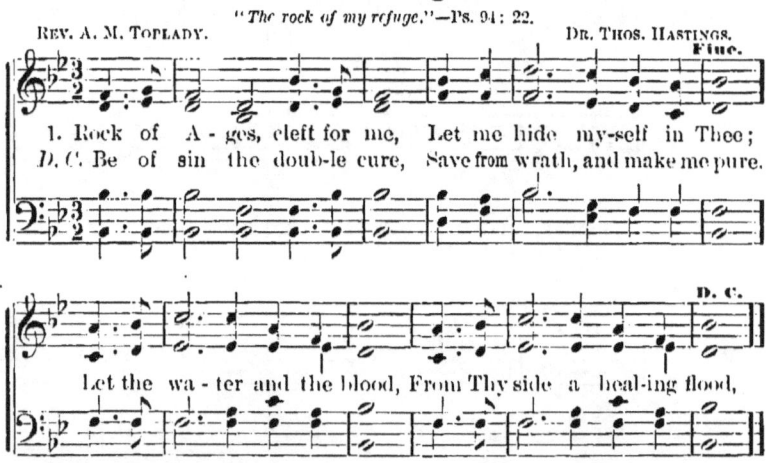

1. Rock of A-ges, cleft for me, Let me hide my-self in Thee;
D. C. Be of sin the doub-le cure, Save from wrath, and make me pure.

Let the wa-ter and the blood, From Thy side a heal-ing flood,

2 Should my tears forever flow,
  Should my zeal no languor know,
  All for sin could not atone;
  Thou must save, and Thou alone;
  In my hand no price I bring;
  Simply to Thy cross I cling.

3 While I draw this fleeting breath,
  When mine eyelids close in death,
  When I rise to worlds unknown,
  See Thee on Thy judgment throne—
  Rock of Ages, cleft for me,
  Let me hide myself in Thee.

To the Work. Concluded.

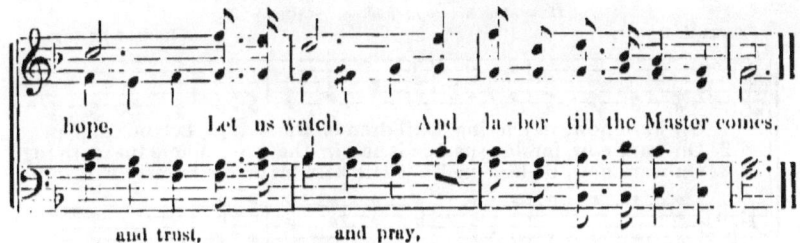

hope, Let us watch, And la-bor till the Master comes.
and trust, and pray,

61. Walking in the Light.

"Come ye, and let us walk in the light of the Lord." —Isa. 2: 5.

S. D. Phelps, D. D.   Robert Lowry.

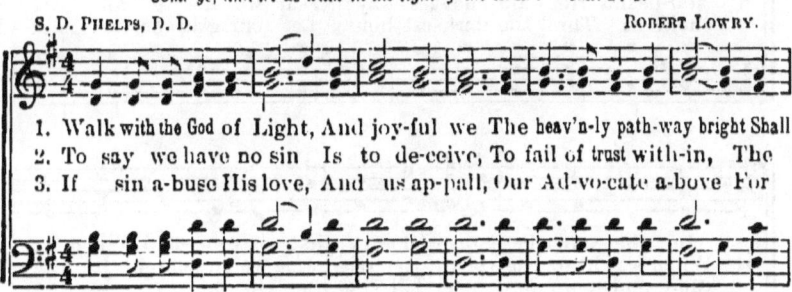

1. Walk with the God of Light, And joy-ful we The heav'n-ly path-way bright Shall
2. To say we have no sin Is to de-ceive, To fail of trust with-in, The
3. If sin a-buse His love, And us ap-pall, Our Ad-vo-cate a-bove For

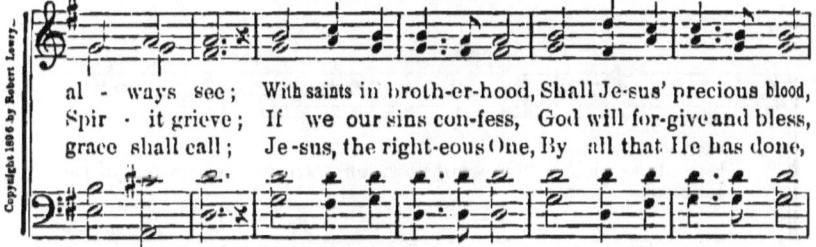

al - ways see; With saints in broth-er-hood, Shall Je-sus' precious blood,
Spir - it grieve; If we our sins con-fess, God will for-give and bless,
grace shall call; Je-sus, the right-eous One, By all that He has done,

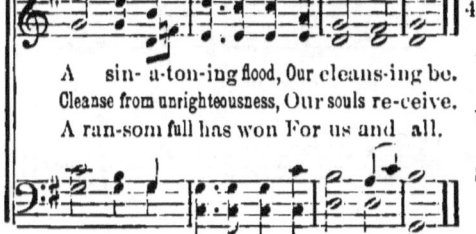

A sin- a-ton-ing flood, Our cleans-ing be.
Cleanse from unrighteousness, Our souls re-ceive.
A ran-som full has won For us and all.

4 Blest they who keep the Word,
Their guide each day,
Walk closely with the Lord,
Know and obey;
Works with true faith combine;
In them the love divine
Shall in perfection shine,
And ne'er decay.

Copyright 1896 by Robert Lowry.

63. Onward! Christian Warriors.

"Hearken to the sound of the trumpet."—JER. 6: 17.

S. F. SMITH, D.D. W. H. DOANE.

Copyright, 1885, by W. H. Doane.

1. On-ward! O Christian Warriors, Wher-e'er the trumpet calls;
   On-ward! the Lead-er sum-mons, Be-yond the shelt'ring walls;
   On-ward! the work a-waits you, Fear not the cold world's frown,
   Arm for the glo-rious con-flict, Then wear the vic-tor's crown.

2. On-ward! with lov-ing pur-pose, Where crime and sor-row reign;
   On-ward! like men in ear-nest, On-ward! with heart and brain;
   On-ward! to save the err-ing, To break the bonds of sin;
   On-ward! the lost to res-cue, Gems for Christ's crown to win.

3. On-ward! the bat-tle thick-ens; The Cap-tain's sig-nal see;
   On-ward! to deeds of glo-ry, On-ward! to vic-to-ry;
   On-ward! with God as-sist-ing, Like sol-diers true and brave,
   Till o'er the con-quered for-tress, Sal-va-tion's ban-ner waves.

In Tenderness He Sought Me. Concluded.

brought me to the fold, Wondrous grace that brought me to the fold!

65. Anywhere, Everywhere.

"They went forth and preached everywhere." —MARK 16: 20.

ROBERT M. OFFORD.   ROBERT LOWRY.

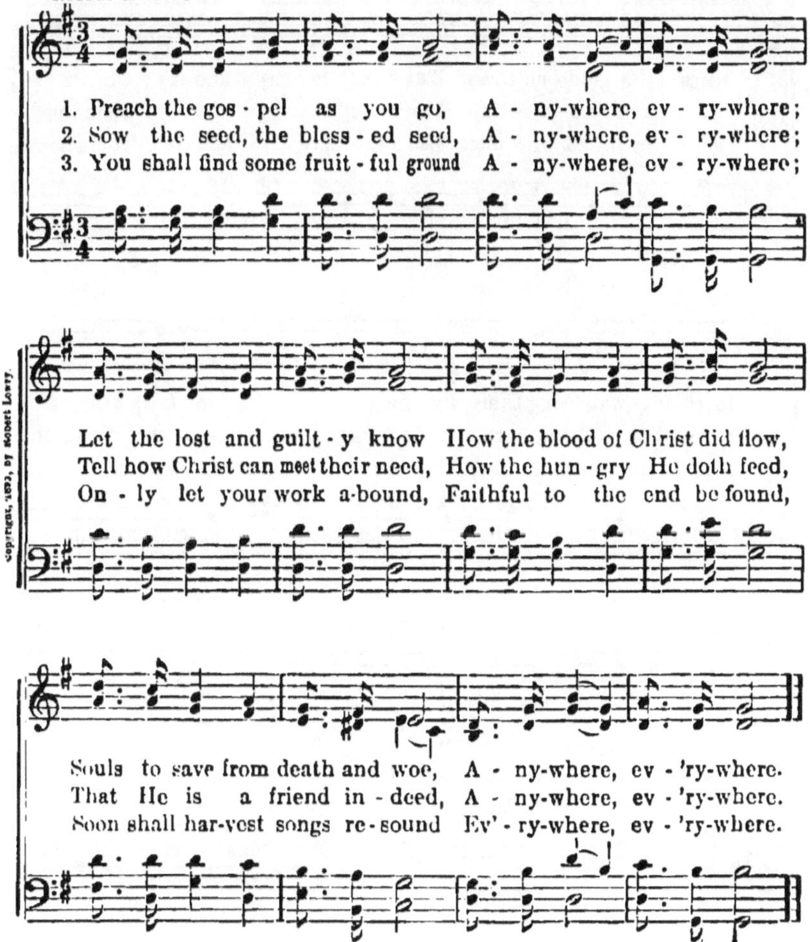

1. Preach the gos-pel as you go, A-ny-where, ev-'ry-where;
2. Sow the seed, the bless-ed seed, A-ny-where, ev-'ry-where;
3. You shall find some fruit-ful ground A-ny-where, ev-'ry-where;

Let the lost and guilt-y know How the blood of Christ did flow,
Tell how Christ can meet their need, How the hun-gry He doth feed,
On-ly let your work a-bound, Faithful to the end be found,

Souls to save from death and woe, A-ny-where, ev-'ry-where.
That He is a friend in-deed, A-ny-where, ev-'ry-where.
Soon shall har-vest songs re-sound Ev'-ry-where, ev-'ry-where.

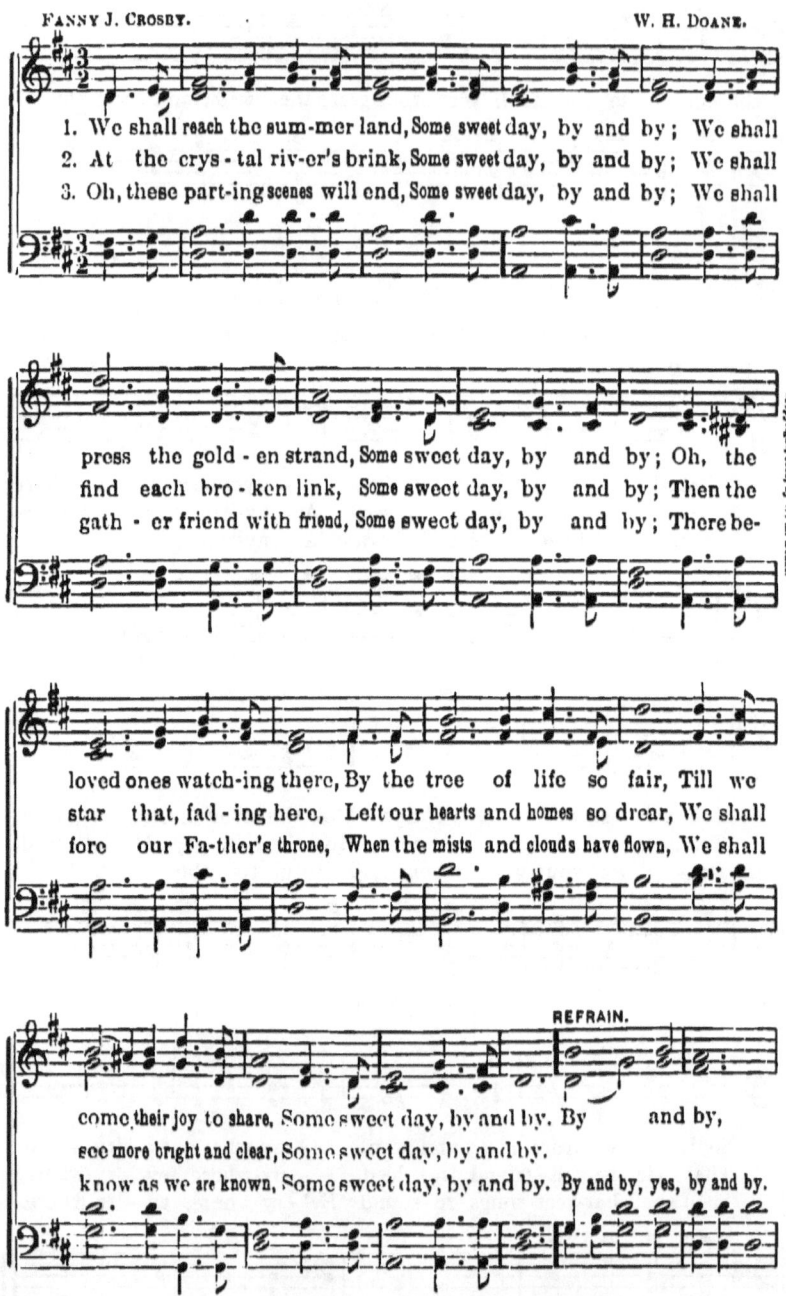

Some Sweet Day, By and By. Concluded.

Some sweet day, We shall meet our lov'd ones gone, Some sweet day, by and by.

---

67 Something for Jesus.

"Lord, what will thou have me to do?"—ACTS 9: 6.

Rev. S. D. PHELPS, D.D. ROBERT LOWRY, by per.

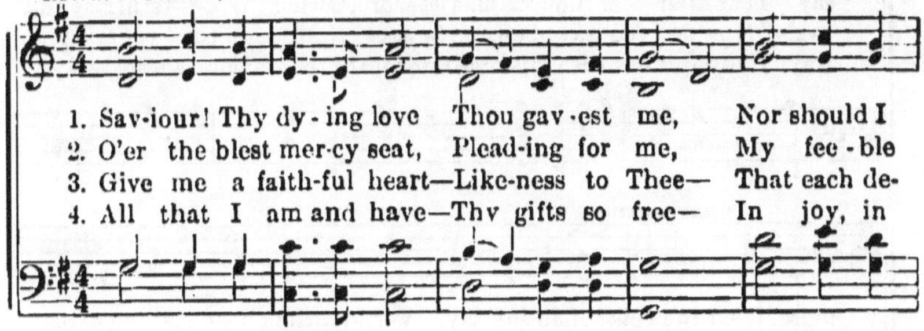

1. Sav-iour! Thy dy-ing love Thou gav-est me, Nor should I
2. O'er the blest mer-cy seat, Plead-ing for me, My fee-ble
3. Give me a faith-ful heart—Like-ness to Thee— That each de-
4. All that I am and have—Thy gifts so free— In joy, in

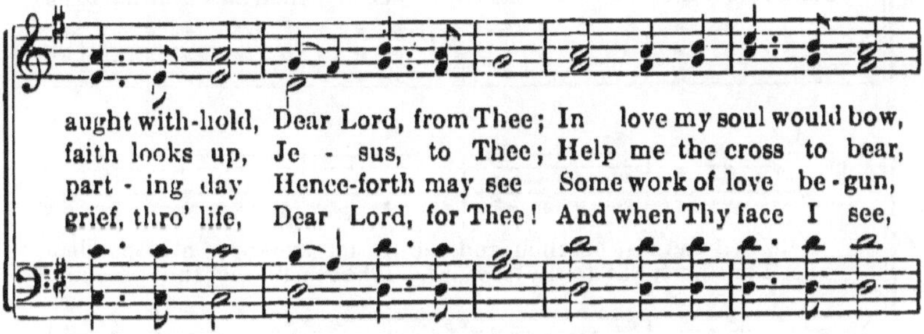

aught with-hold, Dear Lord, from Thee; In love my soul would bow,
faith looks up, Je - sus, to Thee; Help me the cross to bear,
part - ing day Hence-forth may see Some work of love be-gun,
grief, thro' life, Dear Lord, for Thee! And when Thy face I see,

My heart ful-fill its vow, Some offer-ing bring Thee now, Some-thing for Thee.
Thy won-drous love de-clare, Some song to raise, or pray'r, Some-thing for Thee.
Some deed of kind-ness done, Some wan-d'rer sought and won, Some-thing for Thee.
My ran-somed soul shall be, Thro' all e - ter - ni - ty, Some-thing for Thee.

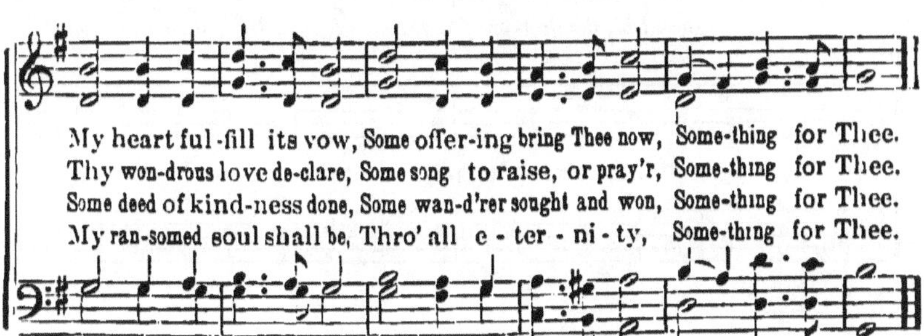

68. Nothing to Pay.

"And when they had nothing to pay he frankly forgave them both."

F. R. H. FRANCES R. HAVERGAL. Arr.

Solo or Choir.

1. Nothing to pay, ah, nothing to pay! Nev-er a word of excuse to say! Year after year thou hast filled the score, Owing thy Lord still more and more. Hear the voice of Je-sus say, "Ver-i-ly, thou hast nothing to pay."
2. Nothing to pay, the debt is so great! What will you do with the awful weight? How shall the way of escape be made? Nothing to pay! yet must be paid! Hear the voice of Je-sus say. "Ver-i-ly, thou hast nothing to pay."
3. Nothing to pay? yes, nothing to pay! Jesus has cleared all the debt a-way; Blotted it out with His bleeding hand! Free and forgiv'n and loved you stand. Hear the voice of Je-sus say, "Ver-i-ly, thou hast nothing to pay."

Congregation.

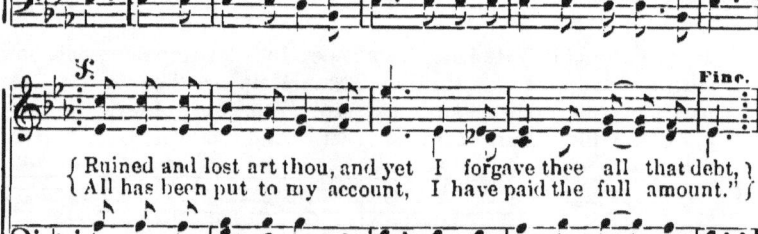

{ Ruined and lost art thou, and yet I forgave thee all that debt, }
{ All has been put to my account, I have paid the full amount." }

"Paid is the debt, the debt-or free! Now I ask thee, lov-est thou me?"

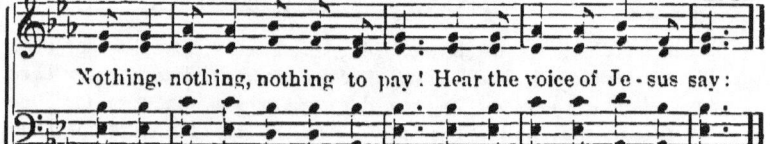

Nothing, nothing, nothing to pay! Hear the voice of Je-sus say:

Loving Kindness. Concluded.

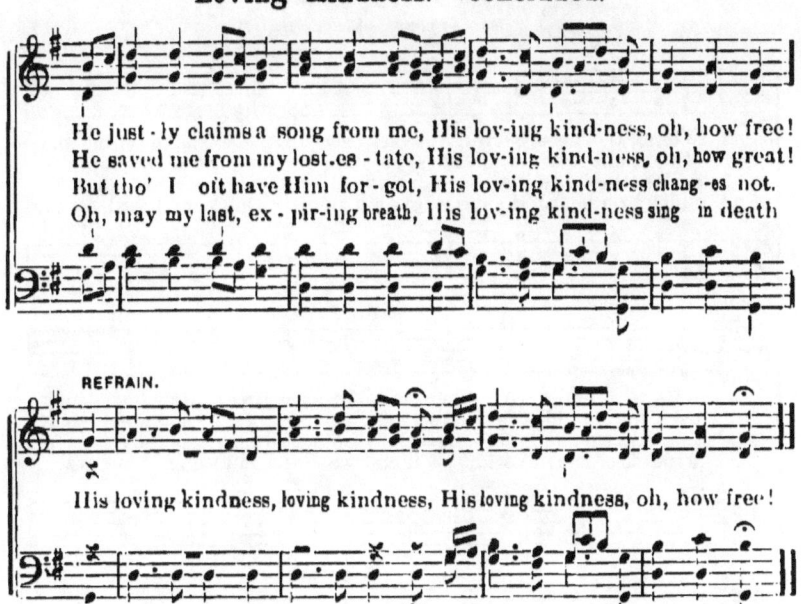

He just-ly claims a song from me, His lov-ing kind-ness, oh, how free!
He saved me from my lost es-tate, His lov-ing kind-ness, oh, how great!
But tho' I oft have Him for-got, His lov-ing kind-ness chang-es not.
Oh, may my last, ex-pir-ing breath, His lov-ing kind-ness sing in death

REFRAIN.

His loving kindness, loving kindness, His loving kindness, oh, how free!

72 Let My Life be Hid with Thee.

"Your life is hid with Christ in God." —COL. 3: 3.

MENDELSSOHN. Arr.

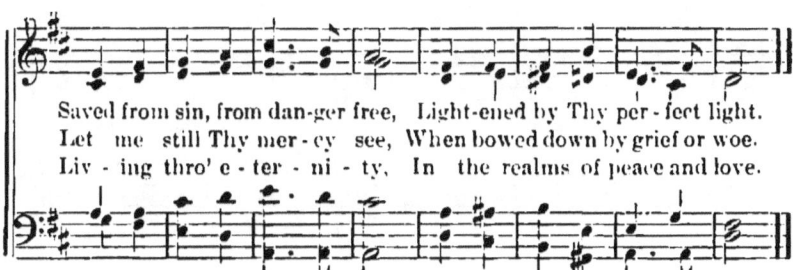

1. Let my life be hid with Thee, Gracious Saviour, Lord of might;
2. Let my life be hid with Thee, When my soul is vexed be-low;
3. Let my life be hid with Thee, Bound with-in Thy life a-bove;

Saved from sin, from dan-ger free, Light-ened by Thy per-fect light.
Let me still Thy mer-cy see, When bowed down by grief or woe.
Liv-ing thro' e-ter-ni-ty, In the realms of peace and love.

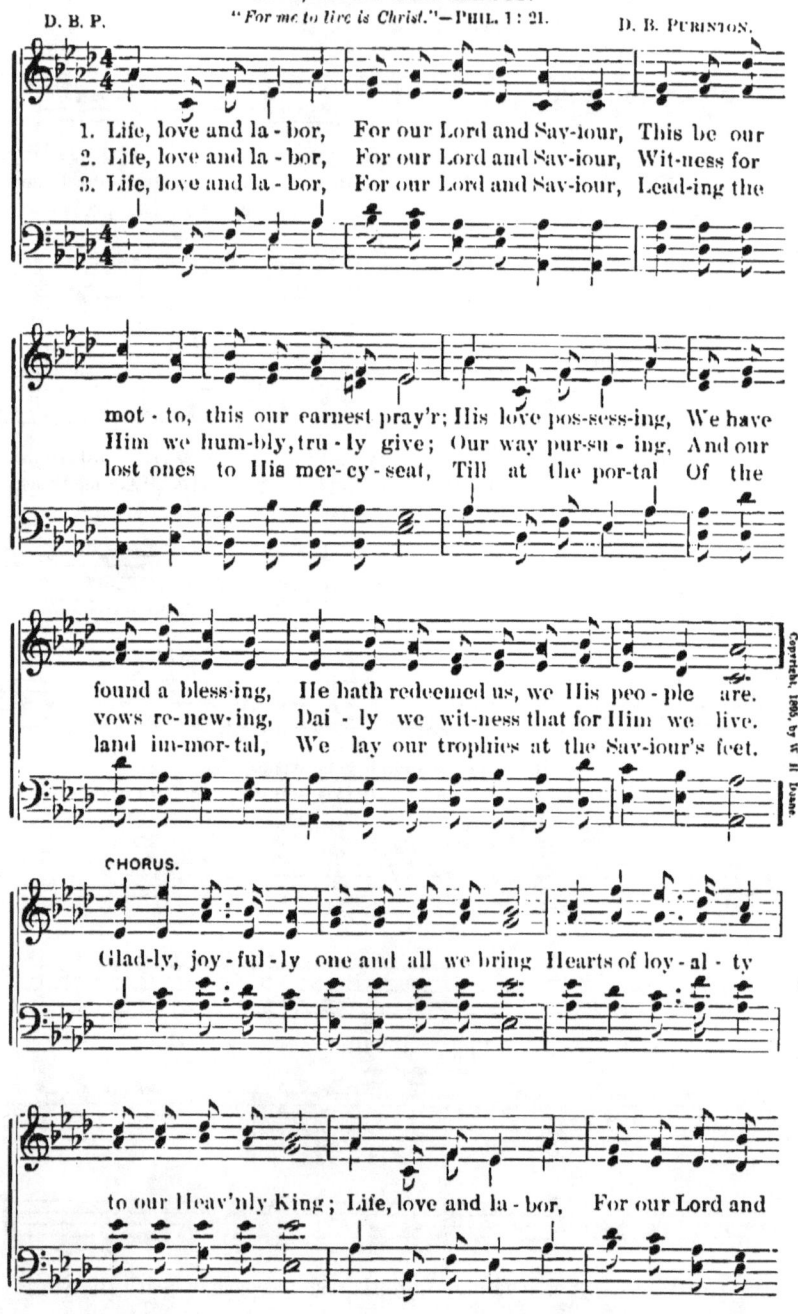

Life, Love and Labor. Concluded.

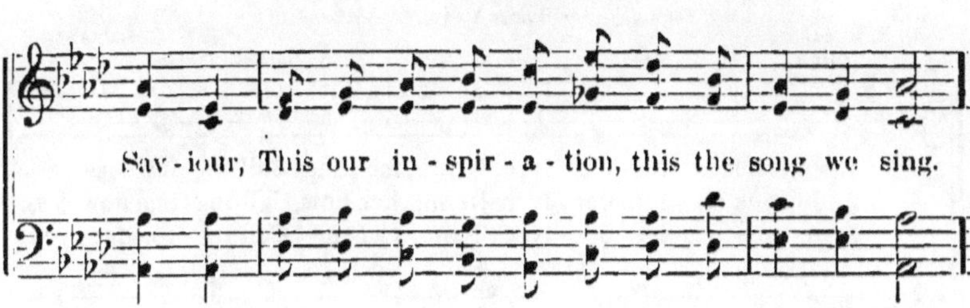

Sav-iour, This our in-spir-a-tion, this the song we sing.

76. Praise to the Trinity.

"Holy, holy, holy, Lord God Almighty."—REV. 4: 8.

IDA SCOTT TAYLOR. W. H. DOANE.

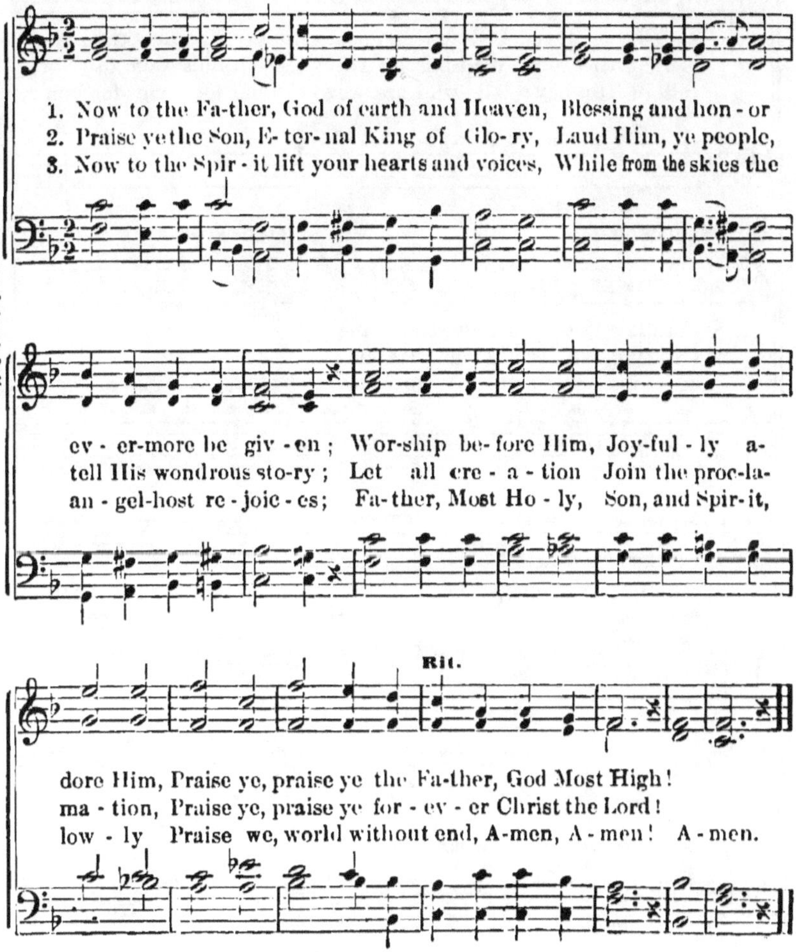

Copyright, 1866, by W. H. Doane.

1. Now to the Fa-ther, God of earth and Heaven, Blessing and hon-or ev-er-more be giv-en; Wor-ship be-fore Him, Joy-ful-ly a-dore Him, Praise ye, praise ye the Fa-ther, God Most High!
2. Praise ye the Son, E-ter-nal King of Glo-ry, Laud Him, ye people, tell His wondrous sto-ry; Let all cre-a-tion Join the procla-ma-tion, Praise ye, praise ye for-ev-er Christ the Lord!
3. Now to the Spir-it lift your hearts and voices, While from the skies the an-gel-host re-joic-es; Fa-ther, Most Ho-ly, Son, and Spir-it, low-ly Praise we, world without end, A-men, A-men! A-men.

81. Refuge.

"He is my refuge, and my fortress." — Ps. 91: 2.

C. WESLEY.   JOS. P. HOLBROOK. By per

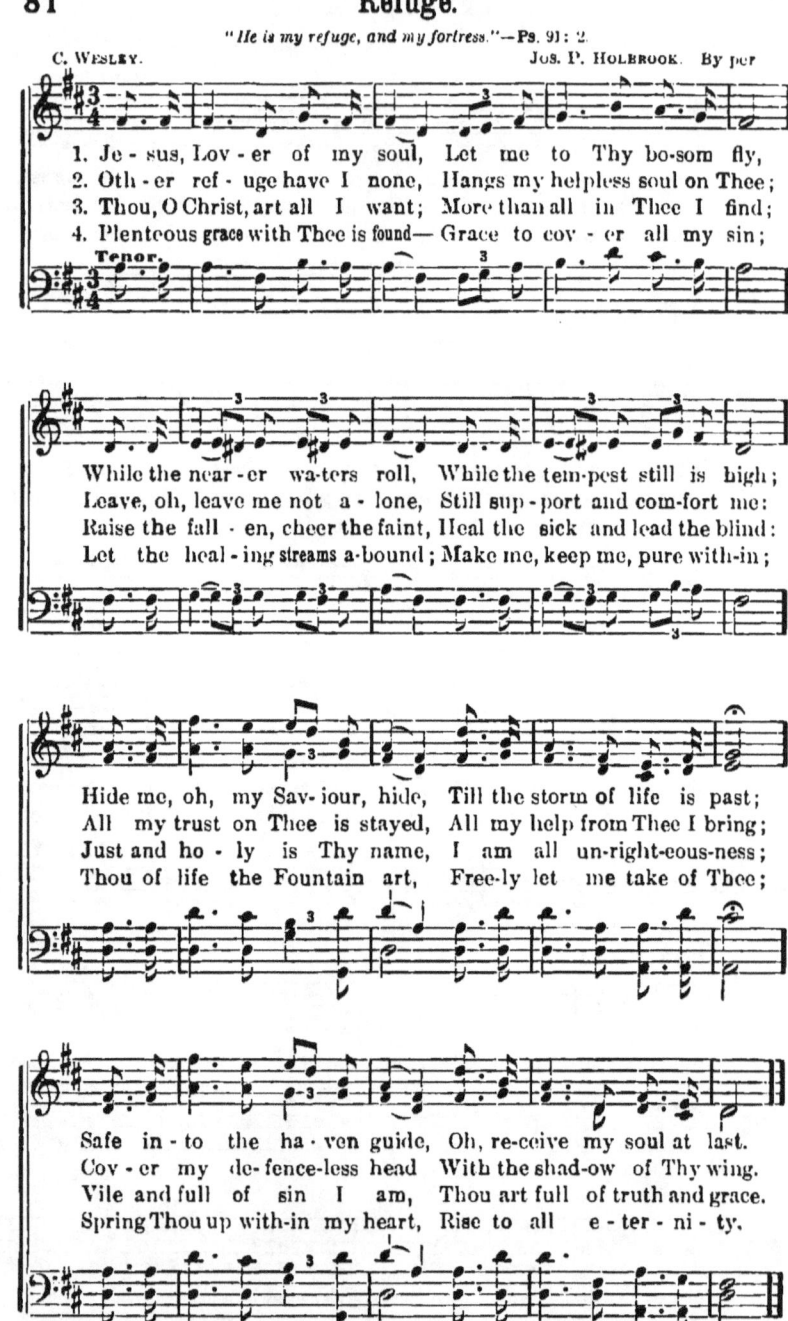

1. Je-sus, Lov-er of my soul, Let me to Thy bo-som fly,
2. Oth-er ref-uge have I none, Hangs my helpless soul on Thee;
3. Thou, O Christ, art all I want; More than all in Thee I find;
4. Plenteous grace with Thee is found— Grace to cov-er all my sin;

While the near-er wa-ters roll, While the tem-pest still is high;
Leave, oh, leave me not a-lone, Still sup-port and com-fort me:
Raise the fall-en, cheer the faint, Heal the sick and lead the blind:
Let the heal-ing streams a-bound; Make me, keep me, pure with-in;

Hide me, oh, my Sav-iour, hide, Till the storm of life is past;
All my trust on Thee is stayed, All my help from Thee I bring;
Just and ho-ly is Thy name, I am all un-right-eous-ness;
Thou of life the Fountain art, Free-ly let me take of Thee;

Safe in-to the ha-ven guide, Oh, re-ceive my soul at last.
Cov-er my de-fence-less head With the shad-ow of Thy wing.
Vile and full of sin I am, Thou art full of truth and grace.
Spring Thou up with-in my heart, Rise to all e-ter-ni-ty.

84. Safe in the Arms of Jesus.

"Underneath are the everlasting arms."—DEUT. 33: 27.

FANNY J. CROSBY.   W. H. DOANE.

1. Safe in the arms of Je - sus, Safe on His gen-tle breast—
2. Safe in the arms of Je - sus, Safe from cor-rod-ing care;
3. Je - sus, my heart's dear ref - uge, Je - sus has died for me;

D. C. *Safe in the arms of Je - sus, Safe on His gen - tle breast—*

Fine.

There by His love o'er - shad - ed, Sweet-ly my soul shall rest.
Safe from the world's temp-ta - tions, Sin can not harm me there.
Firm on the Rock of A - ges, Ev-er my trust shall be.

There by His love o'er - shad - ed, Sweet-ly my soul shall rest.

Hark! 'tis the voice of an - gels, Borne in a song to me,
Free from the blight of sor - row, Free from my doubts and fears;
Here let me wait with pa-tience, Wait till the night is o'er;

D. C. REFRAIN.

O - ver the fields of glo - ry, O - ver the jas - per sea.
On - ly a few more tri - als, On - ly a few more tears.
Wait till I see the morn-ing, Break on the gold-en shore.

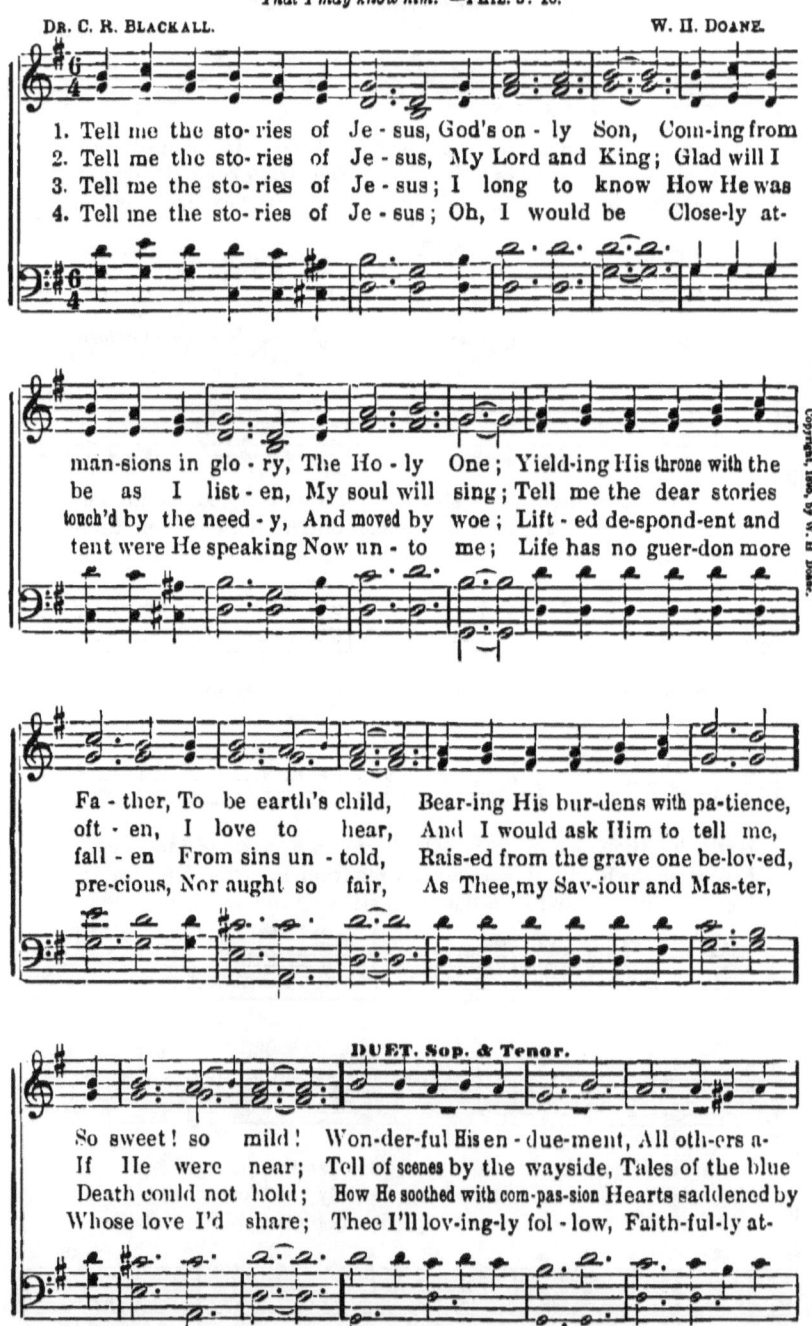

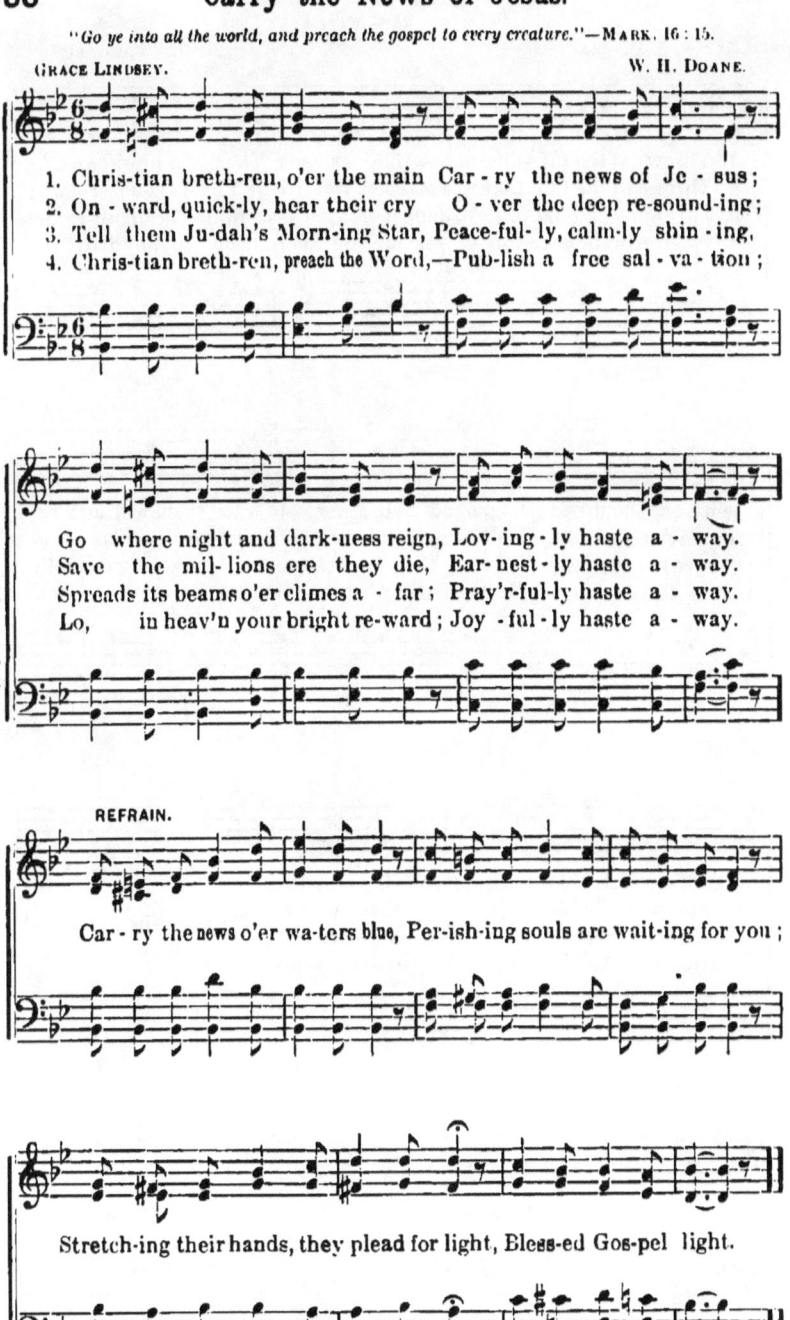

89. Throw Out the Life-Line.

"Lord, save us."—MATT. 8: 25.

REV. E. S. UFFORD.   E. S. U.   Arr. by GEO. C. STEBBINS.

1. Throw out the Life-Line across the dark wave, There is a brother whom some one should save; Some-bod-y's brother! oh, who, then, will dare To throw out the Life-Line, his per-il to share?
2. Throw out the Life-Line with hand quick and strong; Why do you tarry, why lin - ger, so long? See! he is sink-ing; oh, hast - en to-day And out with the Life-Boat! a-way, then, a-way!
3. Throw out the Life-Line to danger-fraught men, Sinking in anguish where you've nev-er been; Winds of tempta - tion and bil - lows of woe Will soon hurl them out where the dark waters flow.
4. Soon will the sea - son of res-cue be o'er, Soon will they drift to e-ter - ni - ty's shore; Haste, then, my brother, no time for de-lay, But throw out the Life-Line and save them to-day.

CHORUS.

Throw out the Life-Line!

Throw out the Life-Line! Some one is drifting a - way; Throw out the

Copyright, 1890, by The Biglow & Main Co. Used by per.

Throw Out the Life-Line. Concluded.

Life-Line! Throw out the Life-Line! Some one is sinking to-day.

90. Jesus Saviour, Pilot me.

"And immediately the ship was at the land." —JOHN 6:21.

REV. EDWARD HOPPER.   J. E. GOULD.

1. Je - sus, Sav - iour, pi - lot me O - ver life's tem-pest-uous sea; Unknown waves before me roll, Hid-ing rock and treach'rous shoal; Chart and compass come from Thee, Je-sus, Sav-iour, pi-lot me.
2. As a moth - er stills her child, Thou canst hush the o - cean wild; Boist'rous waves o-bey Thy will, When Thou sayst to them, Be still; Wond'rous sov'reign of the sea, Je-sus, Sav-iour, pi-lot me.
3. When at last I near the shore, And the fear - ful break-ers roar, Twixt me and the peaceful rest, Then while lean-ing on Thy breast, May I hear Thee say to me, Fear not, I will pi-lot thee.

Keep Your Covenant With Jesus. Concluded.

For He gave Himself your ransom; Yes, He died, He died for you.

94. Life in His Favor.

"In his favor is life."—Ps. 30 : 5.

REV. JAMES YEAMES.   ROBERT LOWRY.

Copyright 1886, by Robert Lowry.

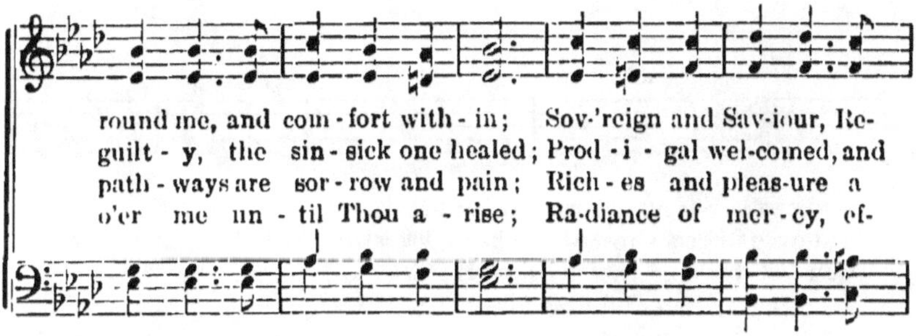

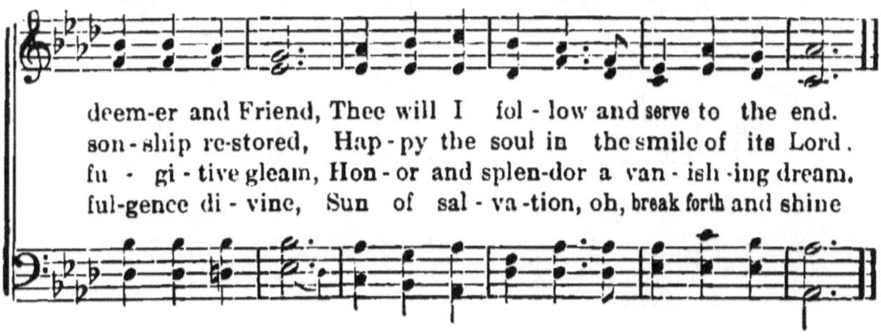

1. Life in His favor! Forgiven all sin, Sunshine around me, and comfort within; Sov'reign and Saviour, Redeemer and Friend, Thee will I follow and serve to the end.
2. Life in His favor! The sentence repealed, Pardoned the guilty, the sin-sick one healed; Prodigal welcomed, and sonship restored, Happy the soul in the smile of its Lord.
3. Life in His favor! All else is but vain, Sin's thorny pathways are sorrow and pain; Riches and pleasure a fugitive gleam, Honor and splendor a vanishing dream.
4. Where can be sunshine If night shroud the skies? Darkness broods o'er me until Thou arise; Radiance of mercy, effulgence divine, Sun of salvation, oh, break forth and shine

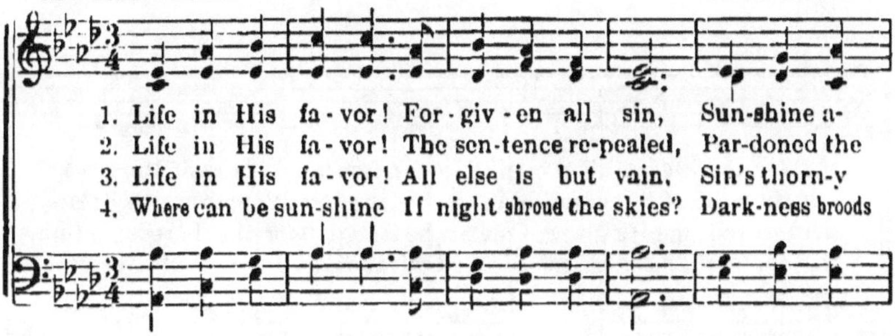

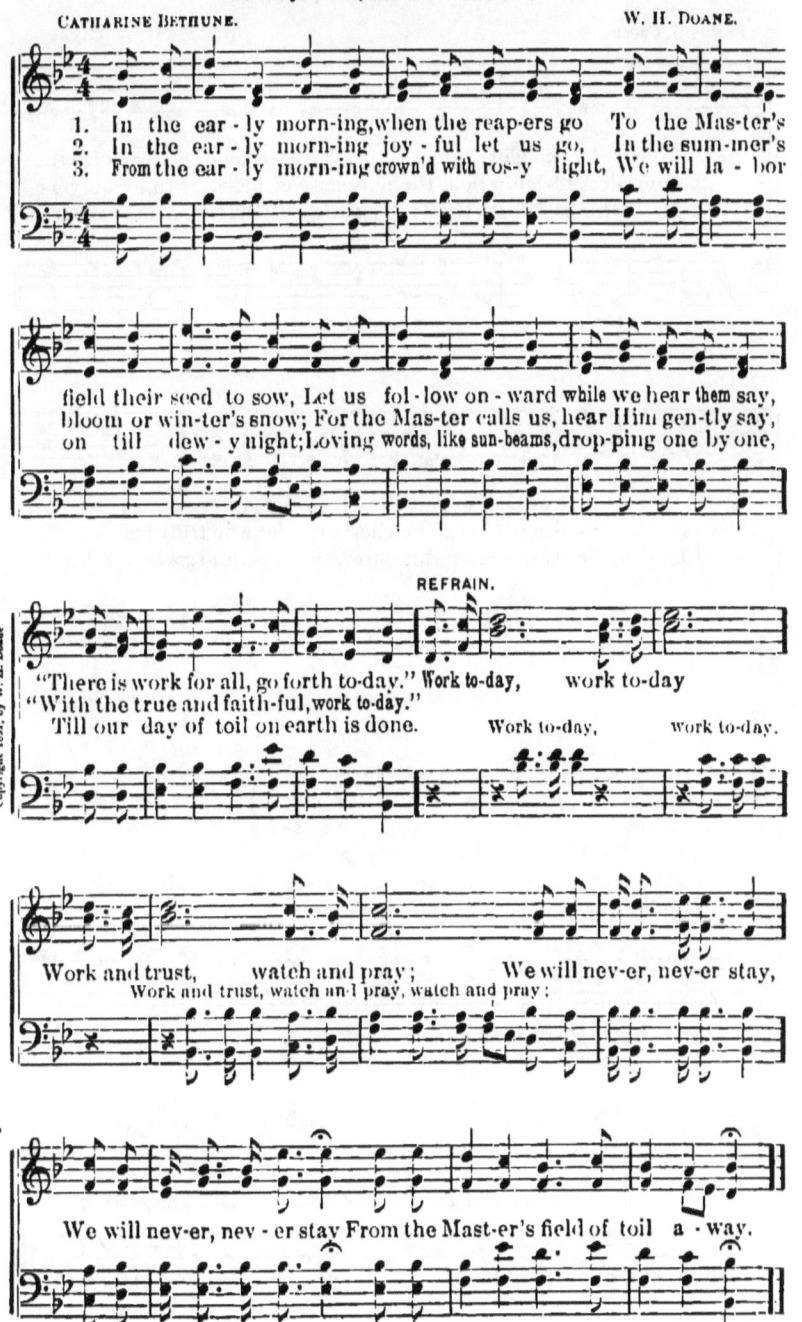

Since I Have Been Redeemed. Concluded.

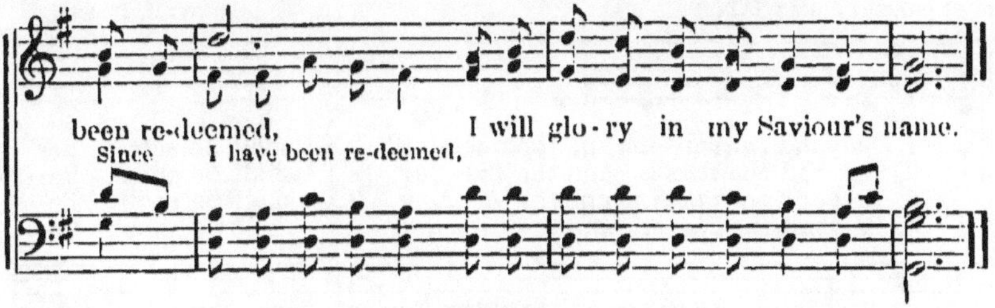

been re-deemed, / Since I have been re-deemed, I will glo-ry in my Saviour's name.

102. My Jesus, as Thou Wilt.

"Not my will, but thine, be done." — LUKE 22: 42.

Tr. by JANE BORTHWICK.   C. M. VON WEBER.

1. My Je-sus, as Thou wilt; Oh, may Thy will be mine; In - to Thy
2. My Je-sus, as Thou wilt; Tho' seen thro' many a tear, Let not my
3. My Je-sus, as Thou wilt, All shall be well for me: Each changing

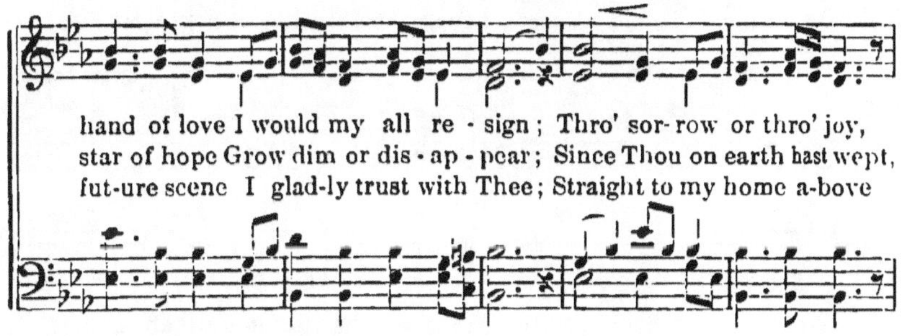

hand of love I would my all re - sign; Thro' sor- row or thro' joy,
star of hope Grow dim or dis - ap - pear; Since Thou on earth hast wept,
fut-ure scene I glad-ly trust with Thee; Straight to my home a-bove

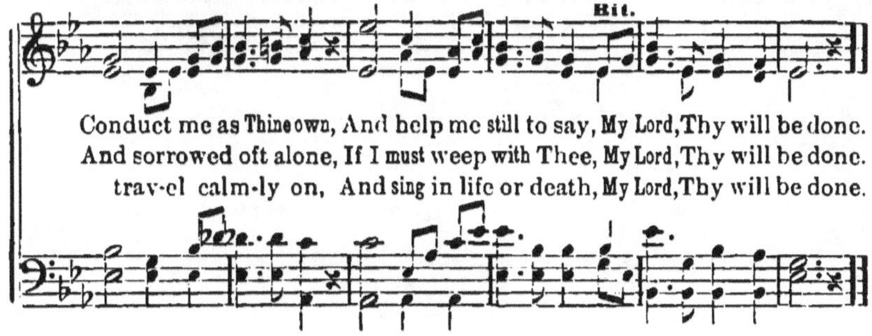

Conduct me as Thine own, And help me still to say, My Lord, Thy will be done.
And sorrowed oft alone, If I must weep with Thee, My Lord, Thy will be done.
trav-el calm-ly on, And sing in life or death, My Lord, Thy will be done.

103. Beyond the Smiling and the Weeping.

"There remaineth therefore a rest to the people of God." — HEB. 4:9.

HORATIUS BONAR, D.D. W. H. DOANE.

1. Be-yond the smil-ing and the weep-ing, I shall be soon; Be-yond the wak-ing and the sleep-ing, Be-yond the sow-ing and the reap-ing, I shall be soon.
2. Be-yond the bloom-ing and the fad-ing, I shall be soon; Be-yond the shin-ing and the shad-ing, Be-yond the hop-ing and the dread-ing, I shall be soon.
3. Be-yond the part-ing and the meet-ing, I shall be soon; Be-yond the fare-well and the greet-ing, Be-yond the pulse's fe-ver beat-ing, I shall be soon.
4. Be-yond the frost-chain and the fe-ver, I shall be soon; Be-yond the rock-waste and the riv-er, Be-yond the ev-er and the nev-er, I shall be soon.

CHORUS.

Love, rest and home! Sweet, sweet home! . . . sweet home! O how sweet it will be there to meet, The dear ones all at home! O how sweet it will be there to meet The dear ones all at home. (at home.)

104. O the Joy to Behold.

"The things which God hath prepared for them that love him."—1 Cor. 2: 9.

WM. STEVENSON.   ROBERT LOWRY.

1. O the joy to be-hold All the glo-ries un-told In the home of the bless-ed a-bove! There the praise I will sing Of my Sav-iour and King, And will tell of His mer-cy and love.
2. As I near that a-bode Brighter will be the road, For the glo-ry a-round me will shine; From the heav-en-ly plains I shall catch the sweet strains, And the joy of the ransomed be mine.
3. And at last I shall meet, In that country so sweet, All the dear ones who've passed on be-fore; There I'll join their glad song, And with heart and with tongue Will the love that has saved us a-dore.

CHORUS.

O the joy of that home, sweet home, . . sweet, sweet home! . . There is naught can com-pare with that cit-y so fair; 'Tis the home of the blessed—my home.

home, sweet home,   home, sweet home!

Copyright, 1895, by Robert Lowry.

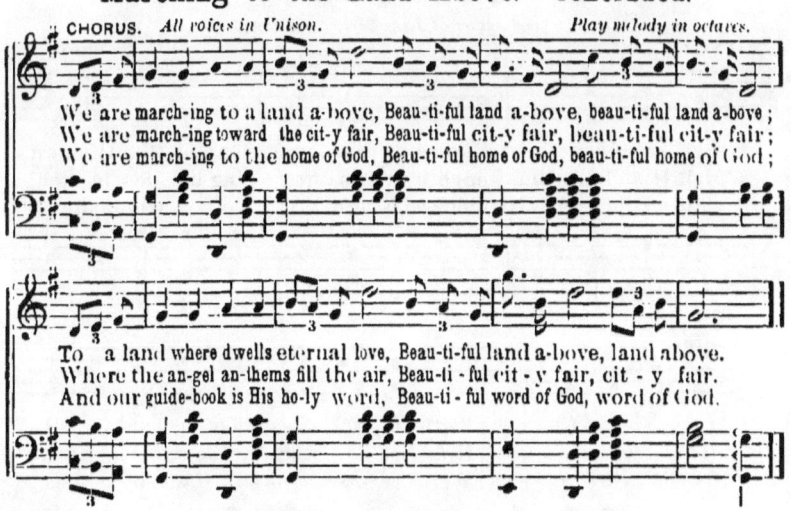

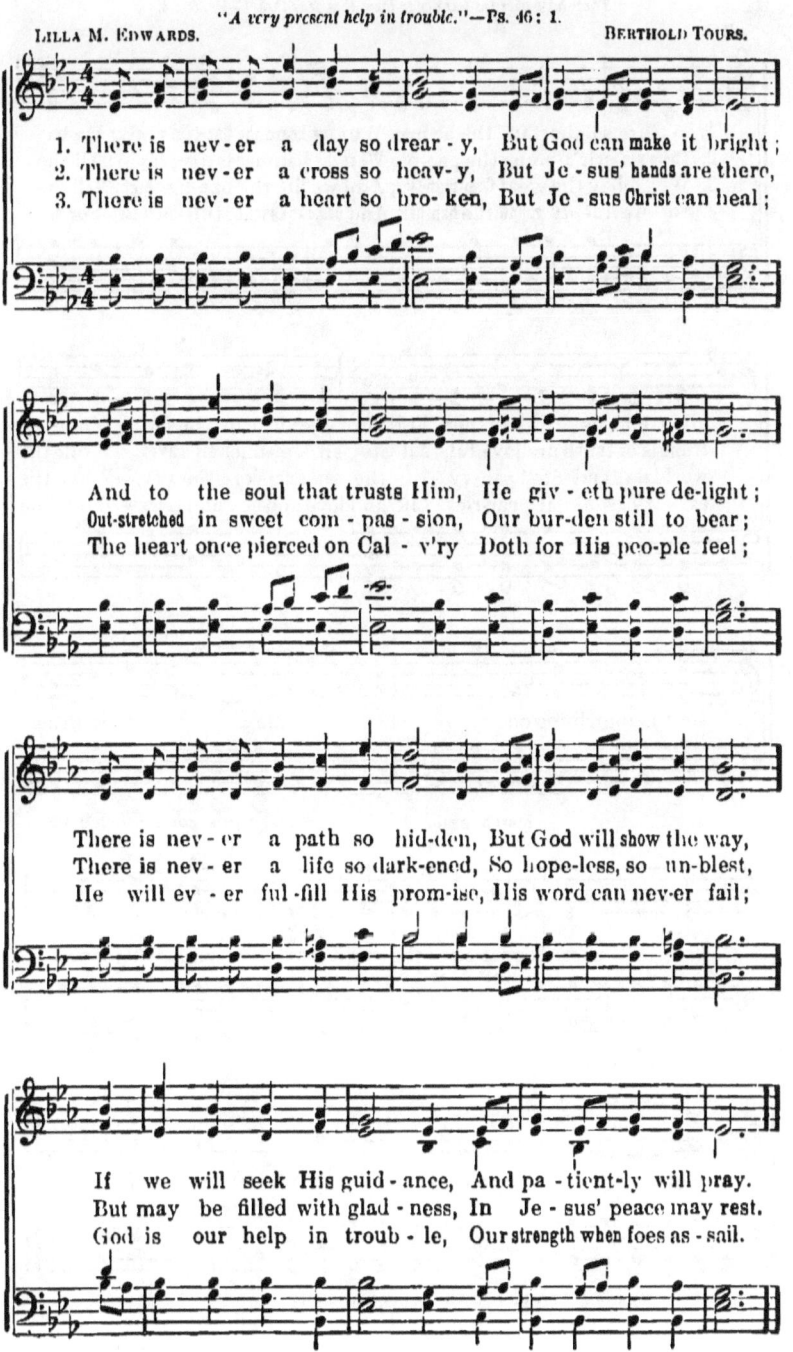

112. Call for Workers.

"The work is great."—1 Chron. 29: 1

Mrs. M. H. Timanus. D. H. W.

1. Hear the in-vi-ta-tion sweeping o'er the land, Come and work for Je-sus in thy youth; Walk in wisdom's pathway, open is the gate, All may en-ter in who keep the truth.
2. Come in youth's bright morning ere the shadows fall, See the Sav-iour waiting now for thee; Trust His loving kindness, hear His gentle voice, "Who-so-ev-er will may come to me."
3. Serve the Lord with gladness, in His love re-joice; Blest are they who do His ho-ly will; He will give thee power, He will give thee strength, And His blessed prom-is-es ful-fill.

REFRAIN.

Hark! the chorus swelling loud and long, "On to vict'-ry at the King's command!" 'Tis the Church of Je-sus, with a mighty voice Calling to the youth of ev-'ry land.

Copyright, 1885, by W. H. Doane.

115. Faith is the Victory.

"The victory that overcometh the world, even our faith."—1 JOHN 5: 4.

JOHN H. YATES.   IRA D. SANKEY.

1. Encamped a-long the hills of light, Ye Chris-tian sol-diers, rise,
2. His ban-ner o - ver us is love, Our sword the word of God;
3. On ev-'ry hand the foe we find Drawn up in dread ar - ray;

And press the bat - tle ere the night Shall veil the glow-ing skies;
We tread the road the saints a - bove With shouts of triumph trod;
Let tents of ease be left be-hind, And on-ward to the fray;

A-gainst the foe in vales be- low, Let all our strength be hurled;
By faith they, like a whirlwind's breath, Swept on o'er ev-'ry field;
Sal - va - tion's hel-met on each head, With truth all girt a - bout,

Faith is the vic - to - ry, we know, That o - ver-comes the world.
The faith by which they conquered Death Is still our shin-ing shield.
The earth shall tremble 'neath our tread, And ech - o with our shout.

CHORUS.

Faith is the vic - to - ry! Faith is the vic - to - ry!
Faith is the vic - to - ry! Faith is the vic - to - ry!

Oh, glo - ri - ous vic - to - ry, That o - ver-comes the world.

Copyright, 1891, by The Bigelow & Main Co. Used by per.

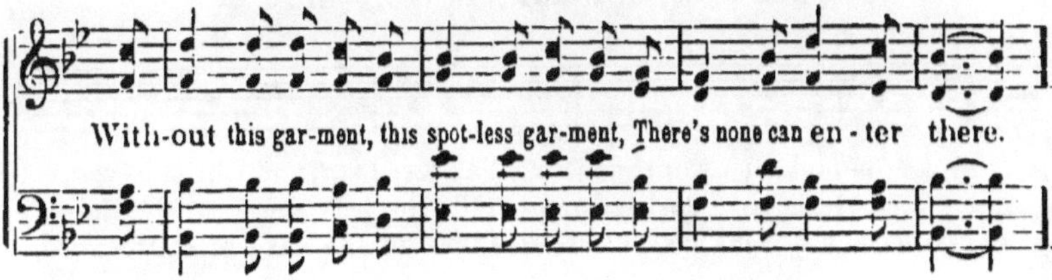

The Wedding Garment. Concluded.

With-out this gar-ment, this spot-less gar-ment, There's none can en-ter there.

118. Still Nearer Thee.

"Draw nigh to God."—JAMES 4: 8.

MARY F. KIRBY.   ROBERT LOWRY.

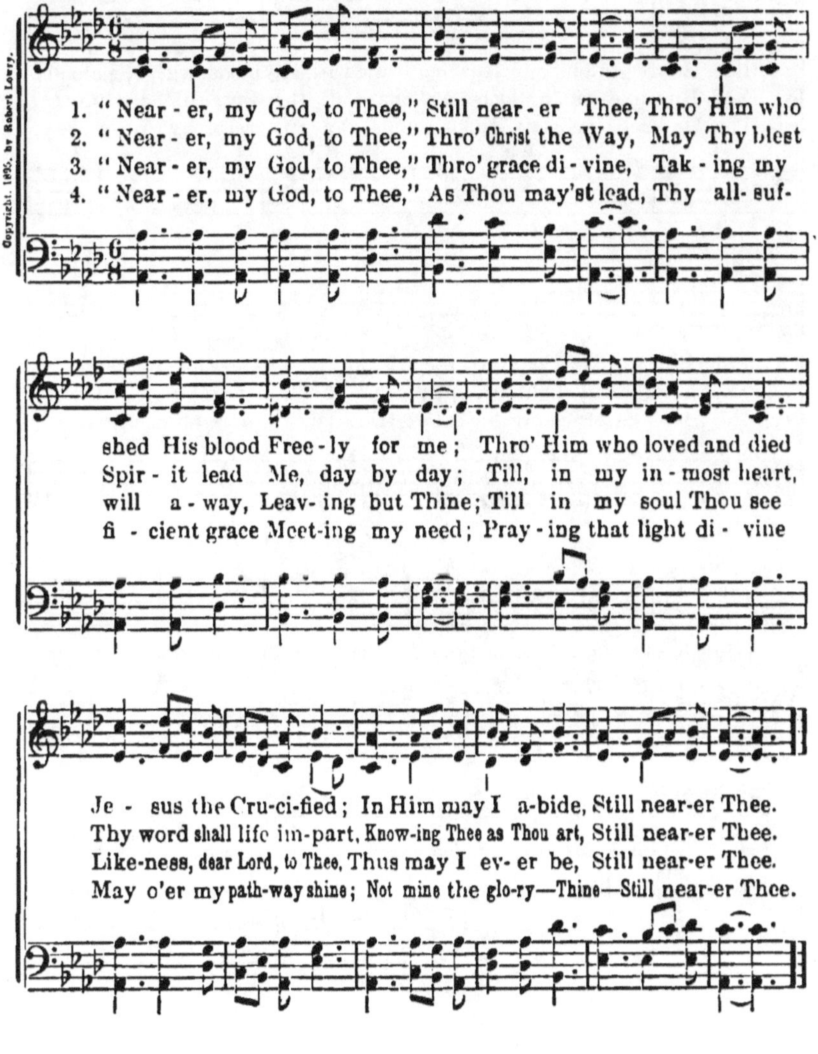

Copyright, 1895, by Robert Lowry.

1. "Near-er, my God, to Thee," Still near-er Thee, Thro' Him who
2. "Near-er, my God, to Thee," Thro' Christ the Way, May Thy blest
3. "Near-er, my God, to Thee," Thro' grace di-vine, Tak-ing my
4. "Near-er, my God, to Thee," As Thou may'st lead, Thy all-suf-

shed His blood Free-ly for me; Thro' Him who loved and died
Spir-it lead Me, day by day; Till, in my in-most heart,
will a-way, Leav-ing but Thine; Till in my soul Thou see
fi-cient grace Meet-ing my need; Pray-ing that light di-vine

Je-sus the Cru-ci-fied; In Him may I a-bide, Still near-er Thee.
Thy word shall life im-part, Know-ing Thee as Thou art, Still near-er Thee.
Like-ness, dear Lord, to Thee, Thus may I ev-er be, Still near-er Thee.
May o'er my path-way shine; Not mine the glo-ry—Thine—Still near-er Thee.

He's the Saviour of My Soul. Concluded.

Hal - le - lu - jah, hal - le - lu - jah, hal - le - lu - jah, praise the Lord.

---

120 Sweet Moments of Prayer.

"There I will meet with thee, and I will commune."—EXOD. 25: 22.

FANNY J. CROSBY. W. H. DOANE.

1. Here from the world we turn, Je - sus to seek; Here may His lov-ing
2. Come, Ho-ly Com-fort-er, Presence di-vine, Now in our longing
3. Sav - iour, Thy work revive, Here may we see Those who are dead in

voice Ten-der-ly speak; Je - sus, our dearest friend, While at Thy
hearts Gra-cious-ly shine; O for Thy mighty pow'r, O for a
sin Quickened by Thee; Come to our hearts to-night, Make ev'ry

feet we bend, O, let Thy smile de-scend, 'Tis Thee we seek.
bless-ed show'r, Fill - ing this hallowed hour With joy di - vine.
bur-den light, Cheer Thou our waiting sight, We long for Thee.

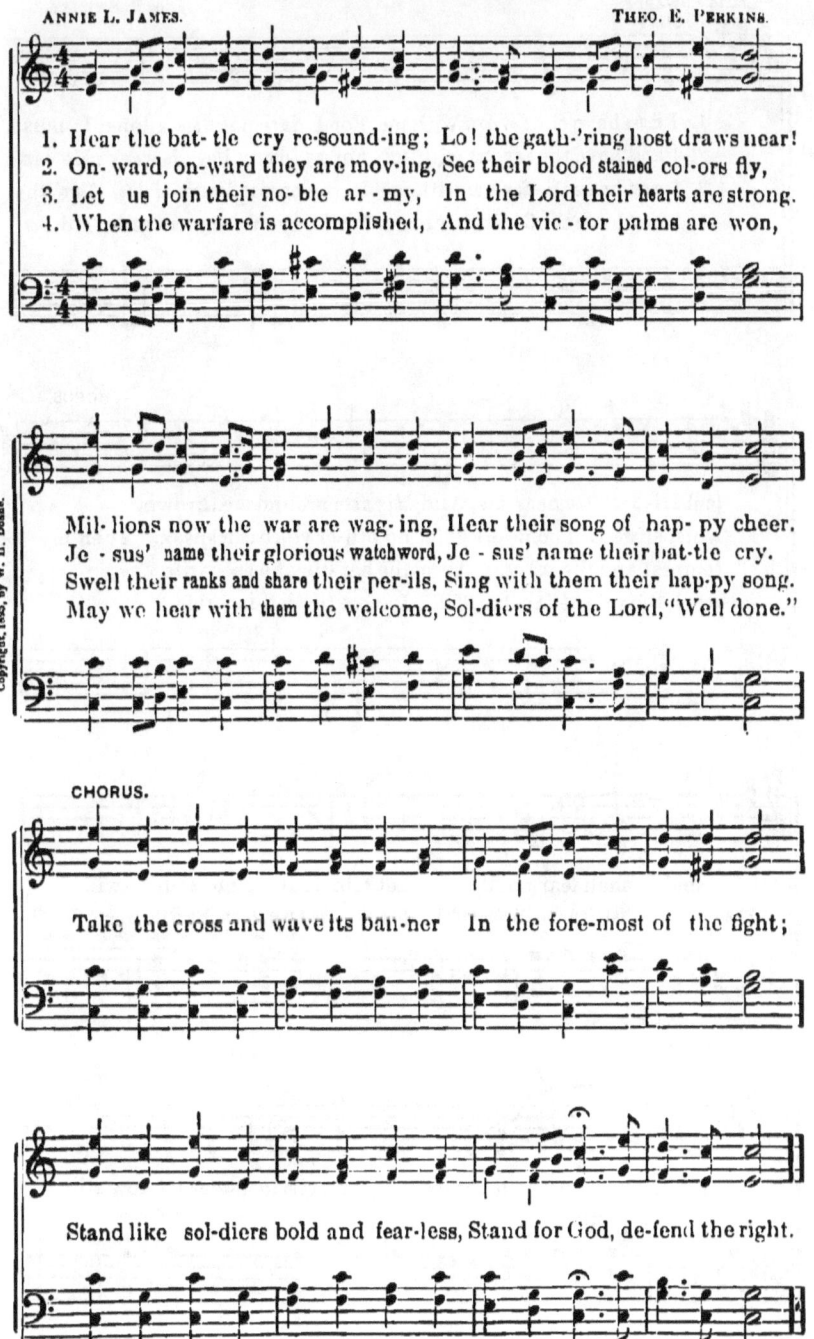

124. Jerusalem the Golden.

"—the holy city, new Jerusalem, coming down from God, out of heaven."—REV. 21:2.

BERNHARD, 1140. Tr. REV. J. M. NEALE.   ALEXANDER EWING.

1. Je-ru-sa-lem the gold-en, With milk and hon-ey blest,
2. They stand, those halls of Zi-on, All ju-bi-lant with song,
3. There is the throne of Da-vid, And there, from care re-leased,
4. O sweet and bless-ed coun-try, The home of God's e-lect!

Be-neath thy con-tem-pla-tion Sink heart and voice op-prest;
And bright with many an an-gel, And all the mar-tyr throng
The song of them that tri-umph, The shout of them that feast;
O sweet and bless-ed coun-try That ea-ger hearts ex-pect!

I know not, O, I know not What joys a-wait us there,
The Prince is ev-er in them, The day-light is se-rene,
And they who, with their Lead-er, Have con-quered in the fight,
Je-sus, in mer-cy bring us To that dear land of rest;

What ra-dian-cy of glo-ry, What light be-yond com-pare.
The past ures of the bless-ed Are decked in glo-rious sheen.
For-ev-er and for-ev-er Are clad in robes of white.
Who art, with God the Fa-ther, And Spir-it, ev-er blest.

Memories of Galilee. Concluded.

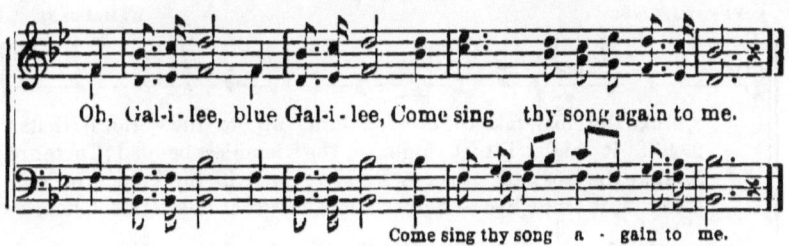

Oh, Gal-i-lee, blue Gal-i-lee, Come sing thy song again to me.
Come sing thy song a - gain to me.

---

128 **Love My Ransom Paid.**

"Herein is love, not that we loved God, but that he loved us."—1 JOHN 4: 10.

FANNY J. CROSBY.   HUBERT P. MAIN.

1. O love, a-maz-ing love, That wounded Thou should'st be For my trans-gres-sions,
2. Thou, like a gen-tle lamb, Wast to the slaugh-ter led, My guilt-y sins were
3. The law my soul con-demns, I have no ref-uge there; The law for ven-geance
4. Yes, 'till my lat-est hour, And with my lat-est breath, Thy won-drous love I'll

CHORUS.

Lord, And sac-ri-ficed for me.
laid Up-on Thy guilt-less head.   Love my ran-som paid, Love my sor-row
calls, But Mer-cy cries for - bear.
sing, E'en thro' the gates of death.   ran-som paid,

bore, Love has o-pened the gate of life; That Love will I a-dore.
sor-row bore,

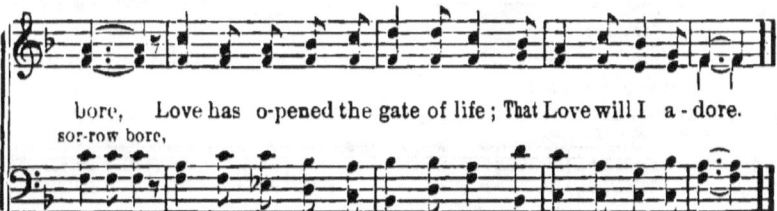

129. Hold it up to the World.

"Go ye into all the world, and preach the gospel to every creature." — MARK 16: 15.

FANNY J. CROSBY.   W. H. DOANE.

Copyright, 1873, by Bigdow & Main.

1. Take the cross, take the cross, hold it up to the world, With its ban-ner of hope by the Sav-iour un-fur!ed; Hold it up, and the lost to its ref-uge may flee Where the dear Sav-iour pleads: I am seek-ing for thee.

2. Lift it high, lift it high, let the friend-less be-hold; There are hearts that will weep when its sto-ry is told; Lift it high, and the poor to its shel-ter may flee Where the dear Sav-iour pleads: I have suf-fered for thee.

3. Take the cross, take the cross, and re-joice in the Lord; Go ye forth, go ye forth in the strength of His word; Hold it up, and the eye of the care-less may see Where the dear Sav-iour pleads: I was wound-ed for thee.

4. O the cross, bless-ed cross, with the blood crim-son tide Like a riv-er of love flow-ing down from its side! To the cross all may come; hold it up, and pro-claim Here is par-don and peace thro' a Sav-iour's dear name.

CHORUS.

Hold it up to the world, Hold it up to the Hold it upward, Hold it upward, Hold it upward, Hold it

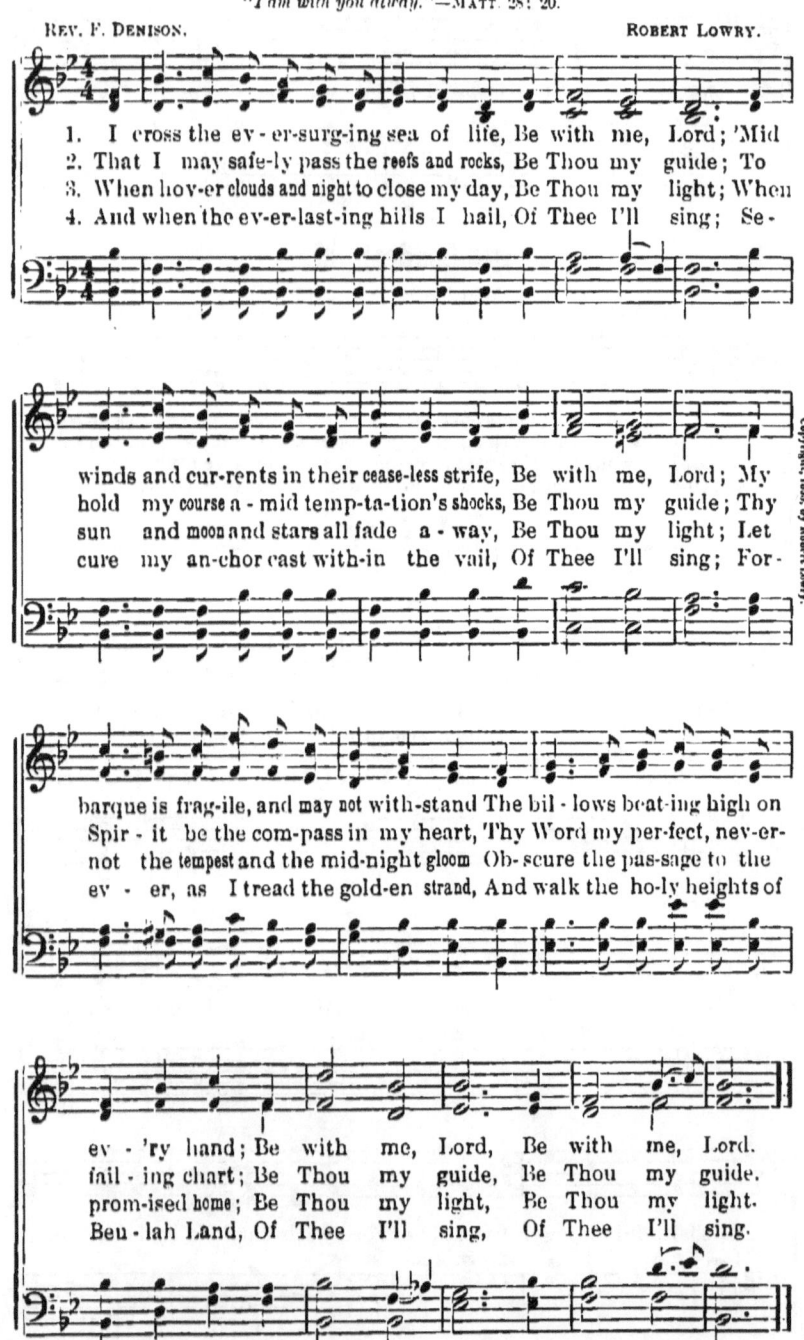

133. In the Cross of Christ.

"God forbid that I should glory, save in the cross."—GAL. 6: 14.

SIR JOHN BOWRING.   ITHAMAR CONKEY.

1. In the cross of Christ, I glo-ry, Tow'ring o'er the wrecks of time;
2. When the woes of life o'er-take me, Hopes deceive and fears an-noy,
3. When the sun of bliss is beaming, Light and love up-on my way,
4. Bane and blessing, pain and pleasure, By the cross are sanc - ti - fied;

All the light of sa - cred story   Gathers round its head sublime.
Nev-er shall the cross for-sake me, Lo, it glows with peace and joy.
From the cross the radiance streaming Adds new lus-tre to the day.
Peace is there that knows no measure, Joys that thro' all time a-bide.

134. Jesus is Mine.

—*"for I know whom I have believed."*—2 TIM. 1: 12.

CATHERINE JANE BONAR.   T. E. PERKINS, by per.

1. Fade, fade each earthly joy, Jesus is mine; Break every tender tie,

D. S. Je - sus a - lone can bless;

Fine.   *D. S.*

Je - sus is mine; Dark is the wilderness, Earth has no resting-place,
Je - sus is mine.

2 Tempt not my soul away,
    Jesus is mine;
Here would I ever stay,
    Jesus is mine;
Perishing things of clay,
Born but for one brief day,
Pass from my heart away;
    Jesus is mine.

3 Farewell, ye dreams of night,
    Jesus is mine;
Lost in this dawning light,
    Jesus is mine;
All that my soul has tried
Left but a dismal void,
Jesus has satisfied;
    Jesus is mine.

135. My Faith Looks Up to Thee.

"*Stand fast in the faith.*"—1 COR. 16: 13.

DR. RAY PALMER. DR. LOWELL MASON.

{ Now hear me while I pray; }
{ Take all my guilt a-way; } O let me from this day Be wholly Thine.

2 May thy rich grace impart
Strength to my fainting heart—
    My zeal inspire;
As Thou hast died for me,
O, may my love to Thee,
Pure, warm, and changeless be—
    A living fire.

3 While life's dark maze I tread,
And griefs around me spread,
    Be Thou my Guide;
Bid darkness turn to day,

Wipe sorrow's tears away,
Nor let me ever stray
    From Thee aside.

4 When ends life's transient dream,
When death's cold, sullen stream
    Shall o'er me roll,
Blest Saviour, then, in love,
Fear and distress remove;
O, bear me safe above,
    A ransomed soul!

136. Come, Thou Fount.

"*Give me a blessing.*"—JUDGES 1: 15.

REV. R. ROBINSON.

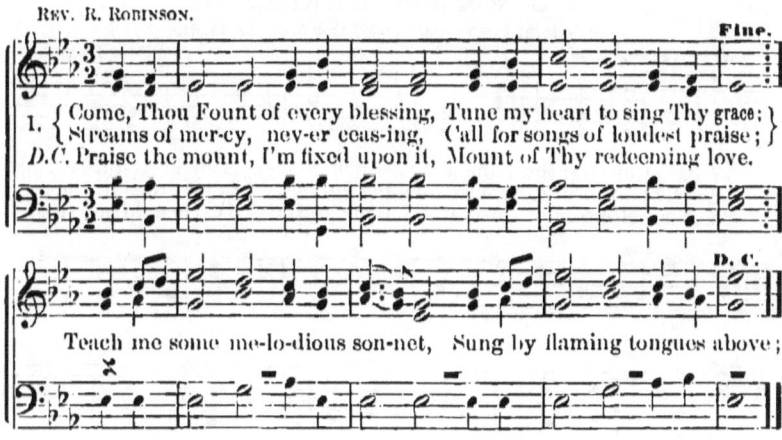

{ Come, Thou Fount of every blessing, Tune my heart to sing Thy grace; }
{ Streams of mer-cy, nev-er ceas-ing, Call for songs of loudest praise; }
D.C. Praise the mount, I'm fixed upon it, Mount of Thy redeeming love.

Teach me some me-lo-dious son-net, Sung by flaming tongues above;

2 Here I raise my Ebenezer;
    Hither by Thy help I'm come;
And I hope by Thy good pleasure,
    Safely to arrive at home;
Jesus sought me when a stranger,
    Wandering from the fold of God;
He, to rescue me from danger,
    Interposed his precious blood.

3 O, to grace how great a debtor
    Daily I'm constrained to be!
Let Thy goodness, like a fetter,
    Bind my wandering heart to Thee;
Prone to wander, Lord, I feel it,
    Prone to leave the God I love;
Here's my heart, O, take and seal it;
    Seal it from Thy courts above.

137. Come, Thou Almighty King.

"Sing praises unto our king."—Ps. 47 : 6.

REV. CHARLES WESLEY. FELICE GIARDINI.

1. Come, Thou almighty King, Help us Thy name to sing, Help us to praise;
Father all glo-ri-ous, O'er all vic-to-ri-ous, Come and reign over us, Ancient of days.

2 Come, Thou incarnate Word,
Gird on Thy mighty sword;
Our prayer attend;
Come, and Thy people bless,
And give Thy word success:
Spirit of holiness, on us descend.

3 Come, holy Comforter,
Thy sacred witness bear,
In this glad hour;
Thou, who almighty art,

Now rule in every heart,
And ne'er from us depart, Spirit of
power.

4 To the great One in Three,
The highest praises be,
Hence evermore;
His sovereign majesty
May we in glory see,
And to eternity Love and adore.

138. O Worship the King.

—"he is thy LORD; and worship thou him.—Ps. 45: 11.

ROBERT GRANT. F. J. HAYDN.

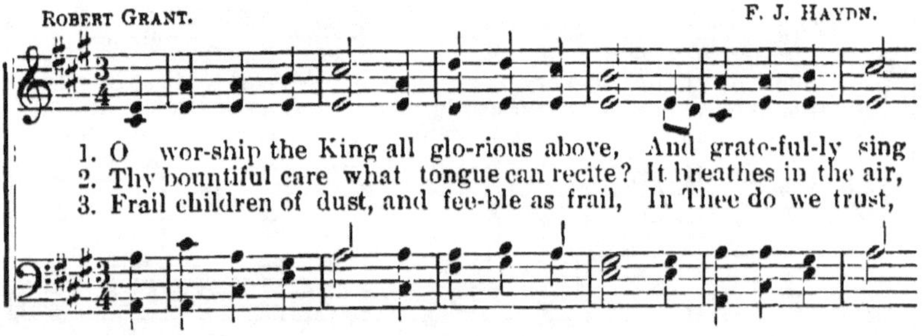

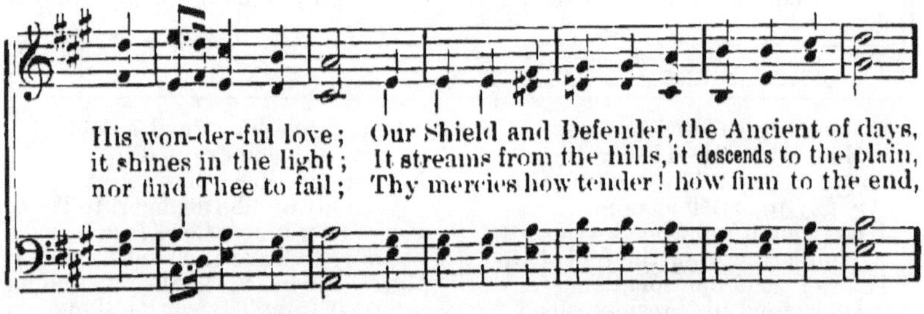

1. O wor-ship the King all glo-rious above, And grate-ful-ly sing His won-der-ful love; Our Shield and Defender, the Ancient of days,
2. Thy bountiful care what tongue can recite? It breathes in the air, it shines in the light; It streams from the hills, it descends to the plain,
3. Frail children of dust, and fee-ble as frail, In Thee do we trust, nor find Thee to fail; Thy mercies how tender! how firm to the end,

O Worship the King. Concluded.

Pa-vil-ion'd in splen-dor and gird-ed with praise.
And sweet-ly dis-tills in the dew and the rain.
Our Mak-er, De-fend-er, Re-deem-er, and Friend.

139   Stand Up for Jesus.

REV. G. DUFFIELD.   *"Quit you like men."*—1 COR. 16:23.   G. J. WEBB.

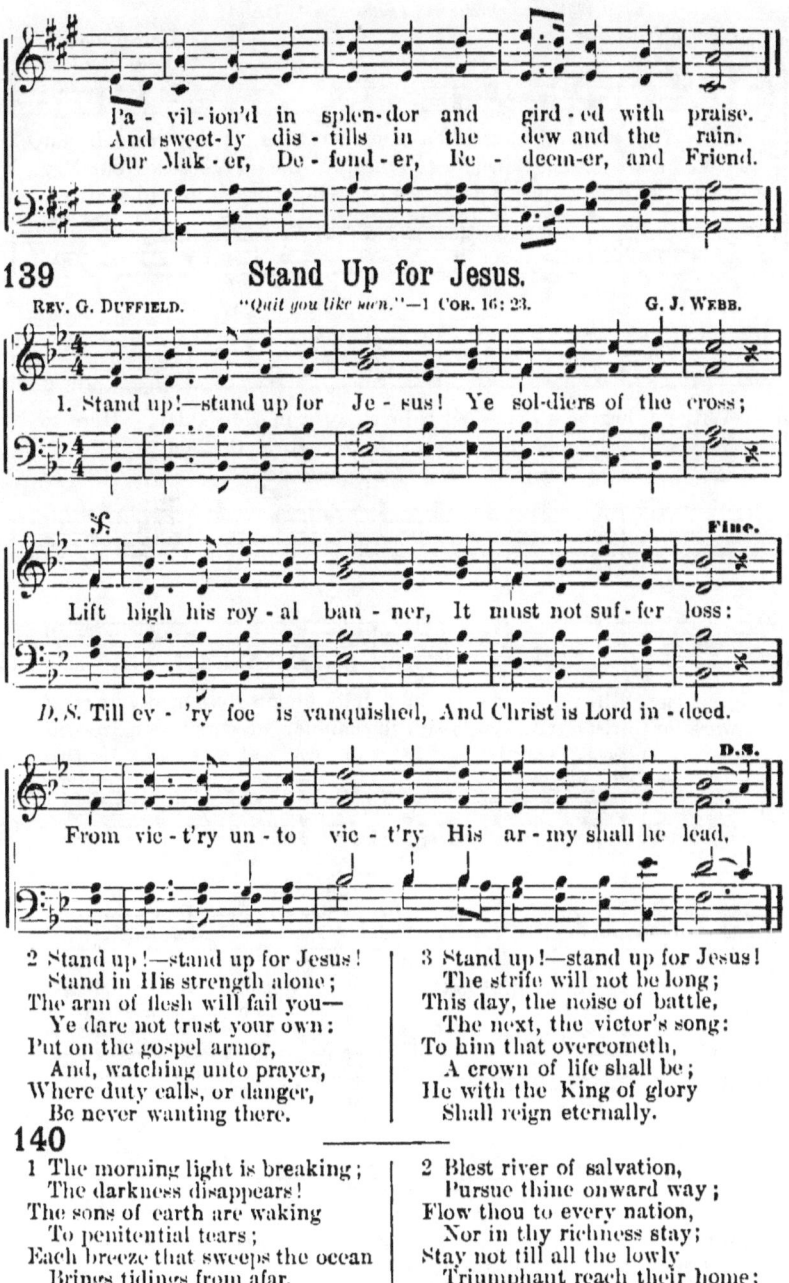

1. Stand up!—stand up for Je-sus! Ye sol-diers of the cross;
Lift high his roy-al ban-ner, It must not suf-fer loss:
D.S. Till ev-'ry foe is vanquished, And Christ is Lord in-deed.
From vic-t'ry un-to vic-t'ry His ar-my shall he lead,

2 Stand up!—stand up for Jesus!
  Stand in His strength alone;
The arm of flesh will fail you—
  Ye dare not trust your own:
Put on the gospel armor,
  And, watching unto prayer,
Where duty calls, or danger,
  Be never wanting there.

3 Stand up!—stand up for Jesus!
  The strife will not be long;
This day, the noise of battle,
  The next, the victor's song:
To him that overcometh,
  A crown of life shall be;
He with the King of glory
  Shall reign eternally.

140

1 The morning light is breaking;
  The darkness disappears!
The sons of earth are waking
  To penitential tears;
Each breeze that sweeps the ocean
  Brings tidings from afar,
Of nations in commotion,
  Prepared for Zion's war.

2 Blest river of salvation,
  Pursue thine onward way;
Flow thou to every nation,
  Nor in thy richness stay;
Stay not till all the lowly
  Triumphant reach their home;
Stay not till all the holy
  Proclaim—"The Lord is come!"
             DR. S. F. SMITH.

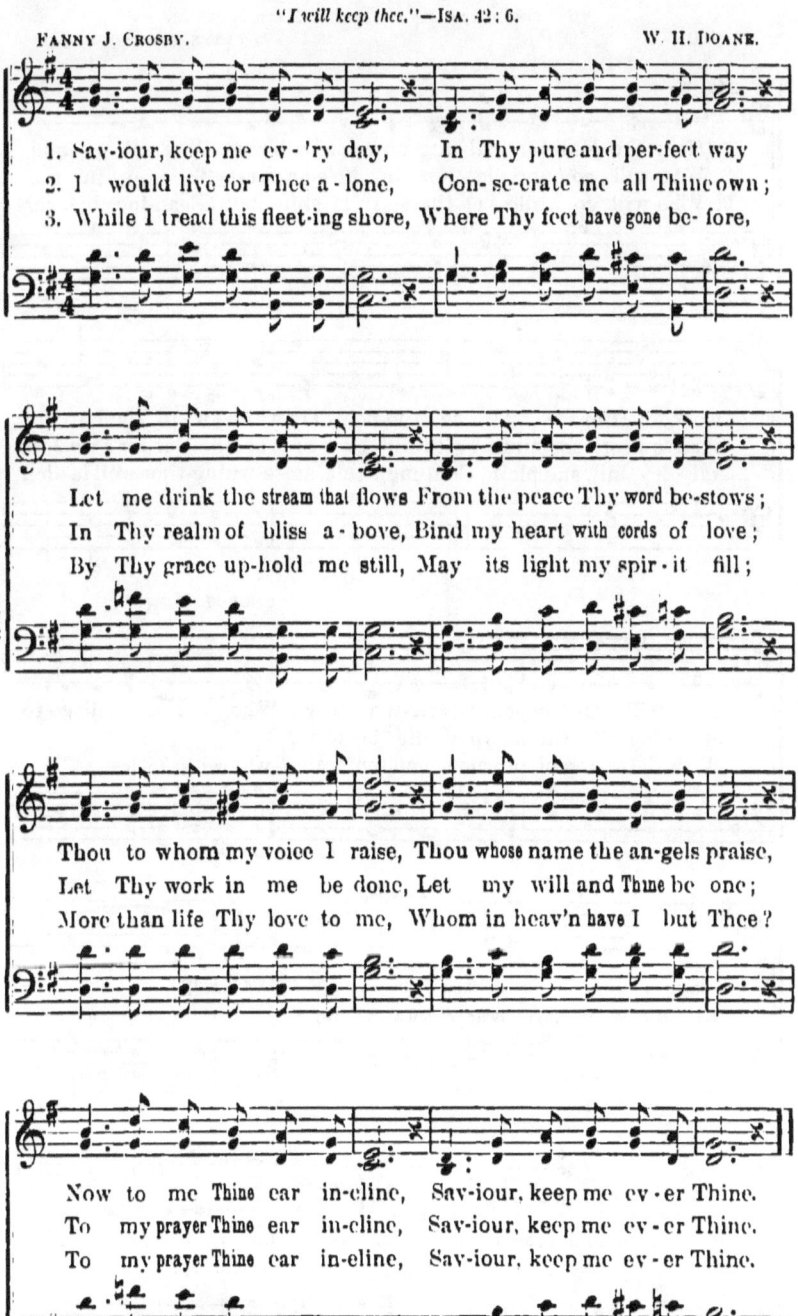

145. Who Will Go To-day?

"Go work to-day in my vineyard." —MATT. 21:28.

F. M. D.
FRANK M. DAVIS, by per.

1. Hear the Mas-ter call-ing now for la-b'rers; Who will go and work for Him to-day? See, the fields are white un-to the har-vest; Who will bear the gold-en sheaves a-way?
2. Who will go and la-bor in life's har-vest, Toil-ing in the shad-ow or the sun, Faith-ful ev-er in the Mas-ter's serv-ice, Striv-ing till the crown of life is won?
3. Who will go while yet the sun is shin-ing, Glean-ing o-ver val-ley, hill, and plain, Com-ing home at e-v'ning-time well la-den With the sheaves of pre-cious gold-en grain?

CHORUS.

Who . . . will go to-day, ... and bear . . . the sheaves a-way? Who will go to-day, and bear the sheaves a-way? Who . . . will go to-day?

Who will go to-day, Bear the sheaves a-way, Bear the sheaves a-way? Who will go to-day.

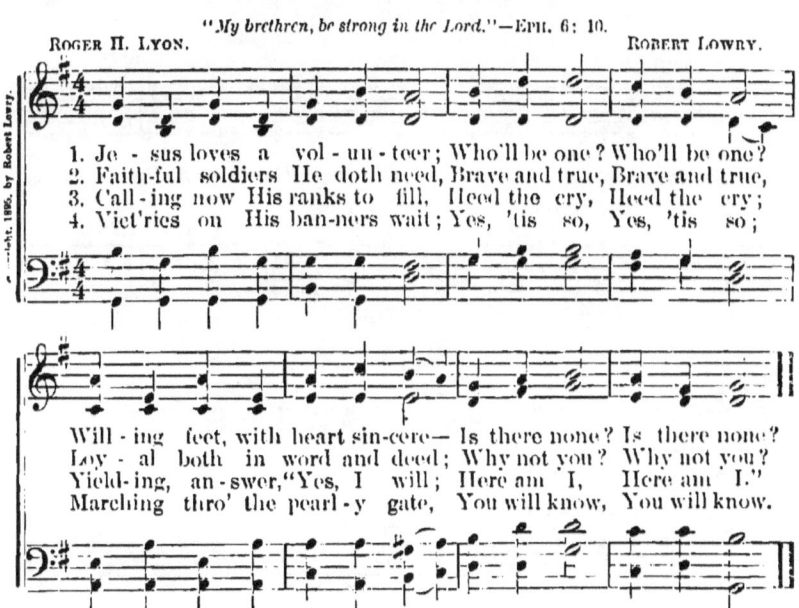

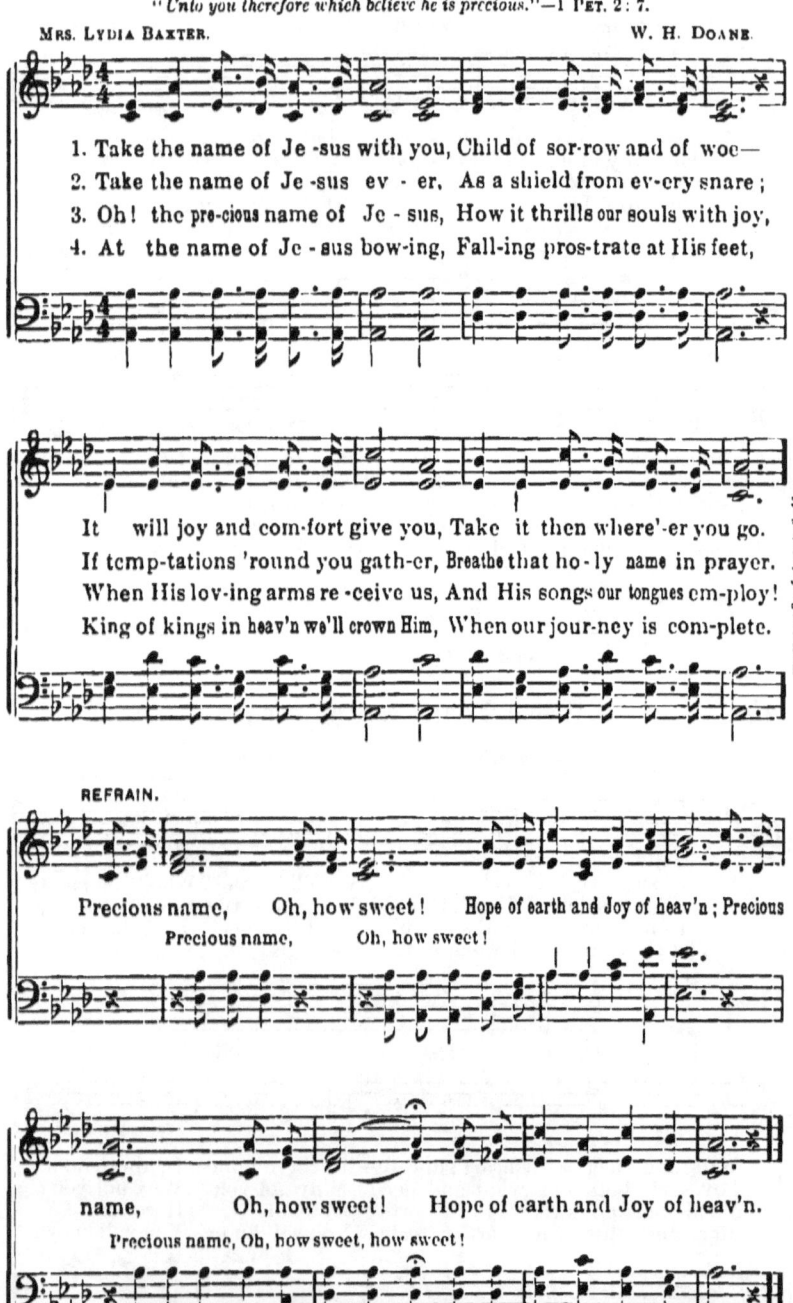

149. The Bible.

"Thy word is a lamp unto my feet."—Ps. 119: 105.

E. O. Excell, by per.

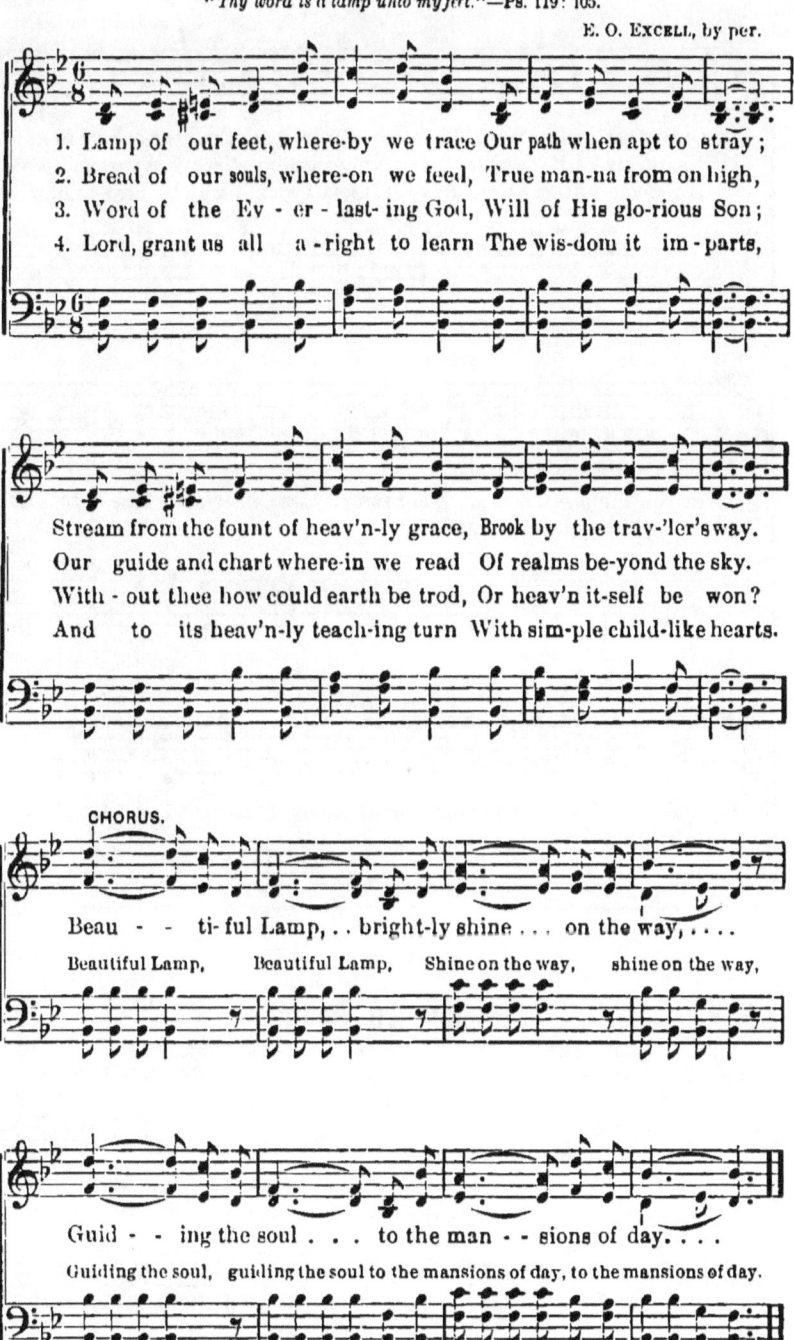

1. Lamp of our feet, where-by we trace Our path when apt to stray;
2. Bread of our souls, where-on we feed, True man-na from on high,
3. Word of the Ev-er-last-ing God, Will of His glo-rious Son;
4. Lord, grant us all a-right to learn The wis-dom it im-parts,

Stream from the fount of heav'n-ly grace, Brook by the trav-'ler's way.
Our guide and chart where-in we read Of realms be-yond the sky.
With-out thee how could earth be trod, Or heav'n it-self be won?
And to its heav'n-ly teach-ing turn With sim-ple child-like hearts.

CHORUS.

Beau - - ti-ful Lamp, .. bright-ly shine ... on the way, ...
Beautiful Lamp, Beautiful Lamp, Shine on the way, shine on the way,

Guid - - ing the soul ... to the man - - sions of day. ....
Guiding the soul, guiding the soul to the mansions of day, to the mansions of day.

150. Nearer My Home.

"Now they desire a better country."—HEB. 11:16.

PHŒBE CARY.　　　　　　　　　　　　　　JOHN M. EVANS.

1. One sweetly solemn thought Comes to me o'er and o'er; I'm near-er home to-day
2. Nearer my Father's house, Where many mansions be; Nearer the great white throne,
3. For e-ven now my feet May stand upon its brink; I may be near-er home,

CHORUS.

Than e'er I've been before.
Near-er the jas-per sea.　　I'm nearer my home, near-er my home, Near-er my
Near-er than now I think.

home to-day; Yes, nearer my home in heav'n to-day, Than ever I've been before.

151. Homeward Bound.

"——they desire a better country, that is, an heavenly."—HEB. 11:16.

REV. W. F. WARREN.　　　　　　　　　　　　REV. J. W. DADMUN.

FINE.

1. { Out on an o-cean all boundless we ride, We're homeward bound, homeward bound;
　　{ Tossed on the waves of a rough, rest-less tide, We're homeward bound, homeward bound;

D. C. Promise of which on us each He bestowed, We're homeward bound, homeward bound.

Homeward Bound.. Concluded.

2 Wildly the storm sweeps us on as it roars,
We're homeward bound, homeward bound;
Look! yonder lie the bright heavenly shores,
We're homeward bound, homeward bound;
Steady, O pilot! stand firm at the wheel,
Steady! we soon shall outweather the gale;
O, how we fly 'neath the loud-creaking sail!
We're homeward bound, homeward bound.

3 Into the harbor of heaven now we glide,
We're home at last, home at last;
Softly we drift on its bright silver tide,
We're home at last, home at last;
Glory to God! all our dangers are o'er,
We stand secure on the glorified shore;
Glory to God! we will shout evermore,
We're home at last, home at last.

152 O Christ, to Thee I Live.

"For to me to live is Christ."—PHIL. 1: 21.

REV. JOHN OTIS BARROWS. ROBERT LOWRY.

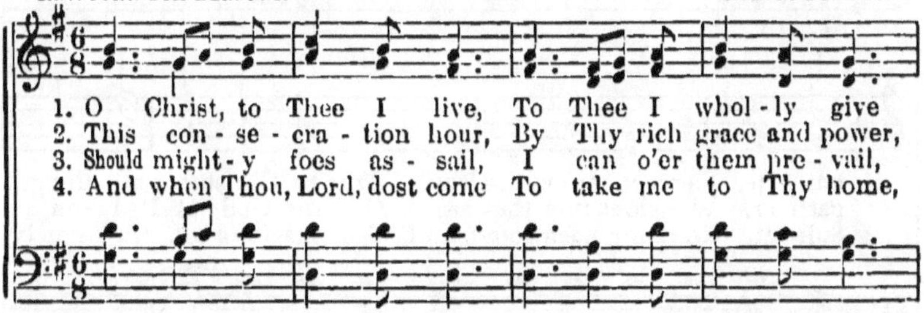

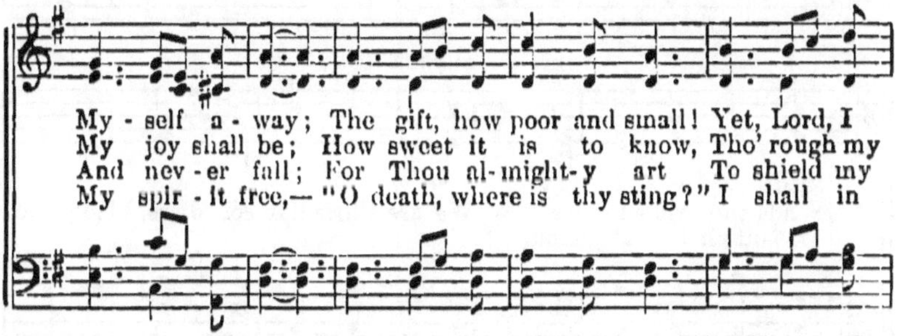

1. O Christ, to Thee I live, To Thee I wholly give
   Myself away; The gift, how poor and small! Yet, Lord, I
   bring Thee all; Before Thy face I fall; Accept, I pray.

2. This consecration hour, By Thy rich grace and power,
   My joy shall be; How sweet it is to know, Tho' rough my
   path below, In all the way I go I walk with Thee!

3. Should mighty foes assail, I can o'er them prevail,
   And never fail; For Thou almighty art To shield my
   open heart From ev-'ry fiery dart; On Thee I call.

4. And when Thou, Lord, dost come To take me to Thy home,
   My spirit free,—"O death, where is thy sting?" I shall in
   triumph sing, As, borne on angel's wing, I rise to Thee.

Copyright, 1883, by Robert Lowry.

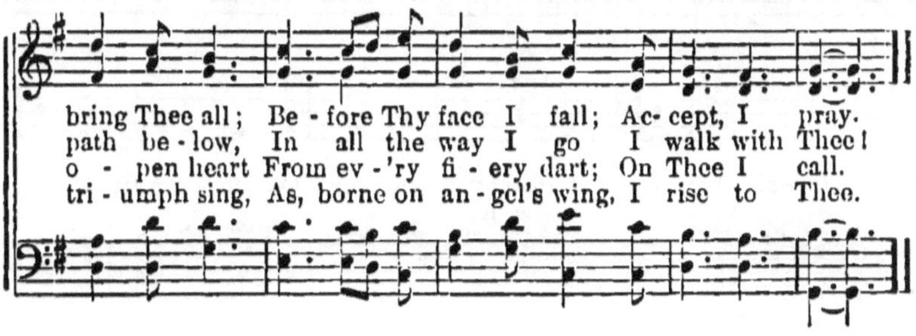

154. True-Hearted, Whole-Hearted.

"I will keep thy precepts with my whole heart."—Ps. 119: 69.

FRANCES R. HAVERGAL.   ROBERT LOWRY.

1. True-heart-ed, whole-heart-ed, faith-ful and loy-al, King of our
2. True-heart-ed, whole-heart-ed, full-est al-le-giance Yield-ing hence-
3. True-heart-ed! Sav-iour, Thou know-est our sto-ry; Weak are the
4. Whole-heart-ed! Sav-iour, be-lov-ed and glo-rious, Take Thy great

lives, by Thy grace we will be; Un-der Thy standard, ex-alt-ed and
forth to our glo-ri-ous King; Val-iant en-deav-or and lov-ing o-
hearts that we lay at Thy feet; Sin-ful and treach-er-ous, yet, for Thy
pow-er and reign Thou a-lone, O-ver our wills and af-fections vic-

Copyright, 1885, by Robert Lowry.

REFRAIN.

roy-al, Strong in Thy strength we will battle for Thee.
be-dience Free-ly and joy-ous-ly now would we bring. True-heart-ed,
glo-ry, Heal them and cleanse them from sin and de-ceit.
to-rious, Free-ly sur-ren-dered, and whol-ly Thine own.

whole-heart-ed, faith-ful and loy-al, Ev-er, O Sav-iour, shall we be to Thee.

155. Truth Triumphant.

"God shall send forth his mercy and his truth."—Ps. 57: 3.

GRACE REED OLIVER.

1. My soul has seen a vi-sion of the con-quest of the world, When
2. No more shall strife and ha-tred bring dis-hon-or to our God, For
3. The des-ert place shall blossom, and the wil-der-ness re-joice, The
4. My soul has heard the tri-umph song that ris-es from the plain, It

Sa-tan and his forc-es from their bat-tle-ments are hurled, And
righteousness, whose work is peace, shall spread her wings a-broad, And
lame shall leap, the blind shall see, the dumb lift up their voice; The
ech-oes and re-ech-oes from the moun-tain-tops a-gain; In

o'er the land the Bi-ble, like a sig-nal flag un-furled, Speaks
they who win the con-quest are the bear-ers of the word, In
floods shall clap their hands, the earth shall make a joy-ful noise, In
grand and might-y cho-rus let us swell the loft-y strain Of

CHORUS.

loy-al-ty to Christ. We shall see the truth so glo-ri-ous O-ver all the earth vic-

to-ri-ous, For the stand-ard lift-ed o-ver us Is loy-al-ty to Christ.

Copyright, 1886, by W. H. Doane.

157. O Thou that Hearest Prayer.

FANNY J. CROSBY.   "*O thou that hearest prayer.*"—Ps. 65: 2.   W. H. DOANE.

1. O Thou that hear-est prayer, Now to my soul draw near,
2. O Thou that hear-est prayer, Je - sus, my bless-ed Lord,
3. O Thou that hear-est prayer, Lead me till life is past,

Bow down Thy gra-cious ear, Turn not a-way. Hear me,
Taught by Thy Ho - ly Word, Trust - ing I come.
Then to Thy - self at last, Lord, take me home.

REFRAIN.

Sav - iour, plead-ing with Thee, Hear me, hear me, O hear Thou me.

158. Father, Whate'er of Earthly Bliss.

ANNE STEELE.   "*He giveth grace unto the lowly.*"—PROV. 3: 34.   DR. LOWELL MASON.

1. Fa-ther, whate'er of earth-ly bliss Thy sov-ereign will de - nies,
2. Give me a calm, a thank-ful heart, From ev-ery mur-mur free;
3. Let the sweet hope that Thou art mine, My life and death at - tend;

Ac - cept-ed at Thy throne of grace, Let this pe - ti-tion rise:
The bless-ings of Thy grace im-part, And make me live to Thee.
Thy pres-ence thro' my jour-ney shine, And crown my jour-ney's end.

Glory to His Name. Concluded.

D. S.

name, Glo-ry to His name.

4 Come to this fountain so rich and sweet;
Cast thy poor soul at the Saviour's feet;
Plunge in to-day, and be made complete;
Glory to His name.

---

162   Rescue the Perishing.

"Lord, save us; we perish." — MATT. 8: 25.

FANNY J. CROSBY.   W. H. DOANE.

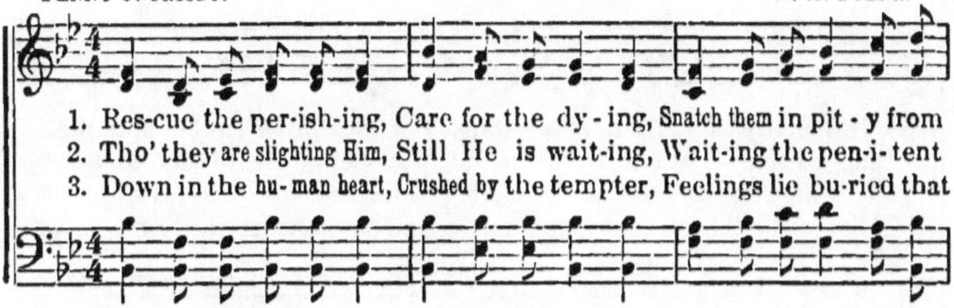

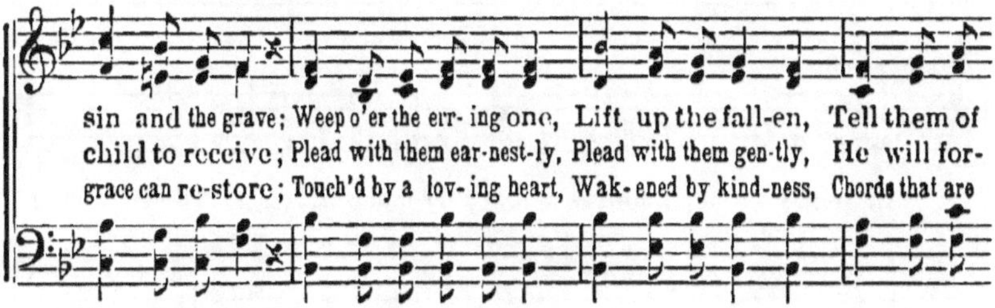

1. Res-cue the per-ish-ing, Care for the dy-ing, Snatch them in pit-y from sin and the grave; Weep o'er the err-ing one, Lift up the fall-en, Tell them of Je-sus, the might-y to save.
2. Tho' they are slighting Him, Still He is wait-ing, Wait-ing the pen-i-tent child to receive; Plead with them ear-nest-ly, Plead with them gen-tly, He will for-give if they on-ly be-lieve.
3. Down in the hu-man heart, Crushed by the tempter, Feelings lie bu-ried that grace can re-store; Touch'd by a lov-ing heart, Wak-ened by kind-ness, Chords that are bro-ken will vi-brate once more.

REFRAIN.

Res-cue the per-ish-ing, Care for the dy-ing;
Je-sus is mer-ci-ful, Je-sus will save.

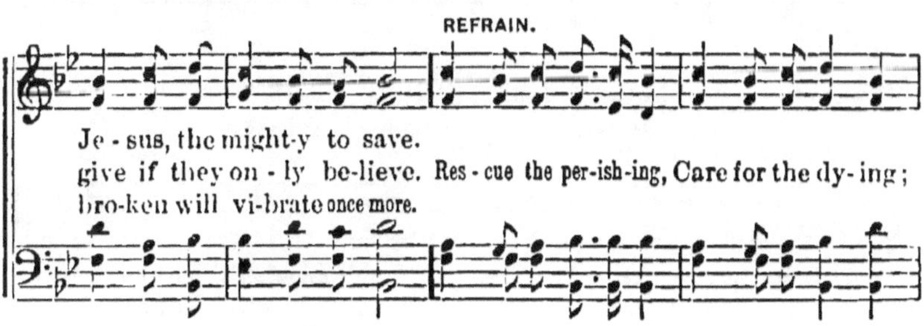

4 Rescue the perishing;
Duty demands it;
Strength for thy labor the Lord will provide;
Back to the narrow way
Patiently win them;
Tell the poor wand'rer a Saviour has died.

Copyright, 1870, by W. H. Doane.

163. Jesus Alone.

"Such trust have we through Christ."—2 Cor. 3:4.

Rev. A. Kenyon. Robert Lowry.

1. My trust is in Jesus alone, For mercy on Him I rely;
2. He died for the guilty and lost, That He our Redeemer might be;
3. Then all that I have I will give, I'll lay it all down at His feet;
4. Tho' vain all my effort must be To rid my poor soul of its woe,

His blood did for sinners atone, For me did He suffer and die.
Salvation—how much it did cost! What mercy He offers to me!
This life for my Saviour I'll live, And count it a privilege sweet.
His grace will bring mercy to me, And pardon most freely bestow.

REFRAIN.

In Jesus alone, in Jesus alone, My trust is in Jesus, in Jesus alone.

Copyright 1886, by Robert Lowry

164. To-day the Saviour Calls.

"If ye seek him, he will be found of you."—2 Chron. 15:2.

S. F. Smith and T. Hastings. Dr. Lowell Mason.

1. To-day the Saviour calls; Ye wanderers, come; O ye benighted souls, Why longer roam!
2. To-day the Saviour calls; O, hear Him now; Within these sacred walls To Jesus bow.

3 To-day the Saviour calls;
 For refuge fly;
 The storm of justice falls,
 And death is nigh.

4 The Spirit calls to-day;
 Yield to His power;
 O, grieve Him not away;
 'Tis mercy's hour.

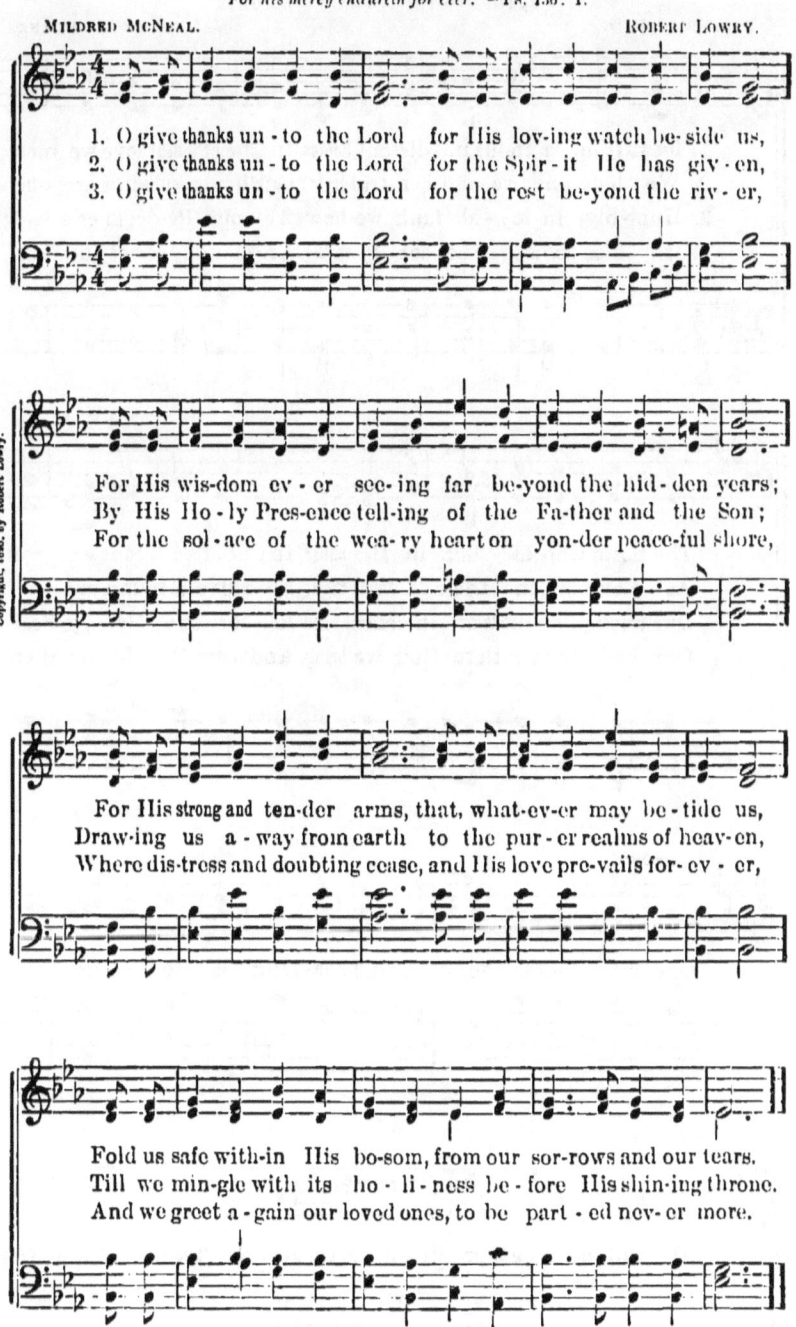

170. By Faith I Draw Nigh.

WM. STEEVNSON. *"By the which we draw nigh."*—HEB. 7: 19. ROBERT LOWRY.

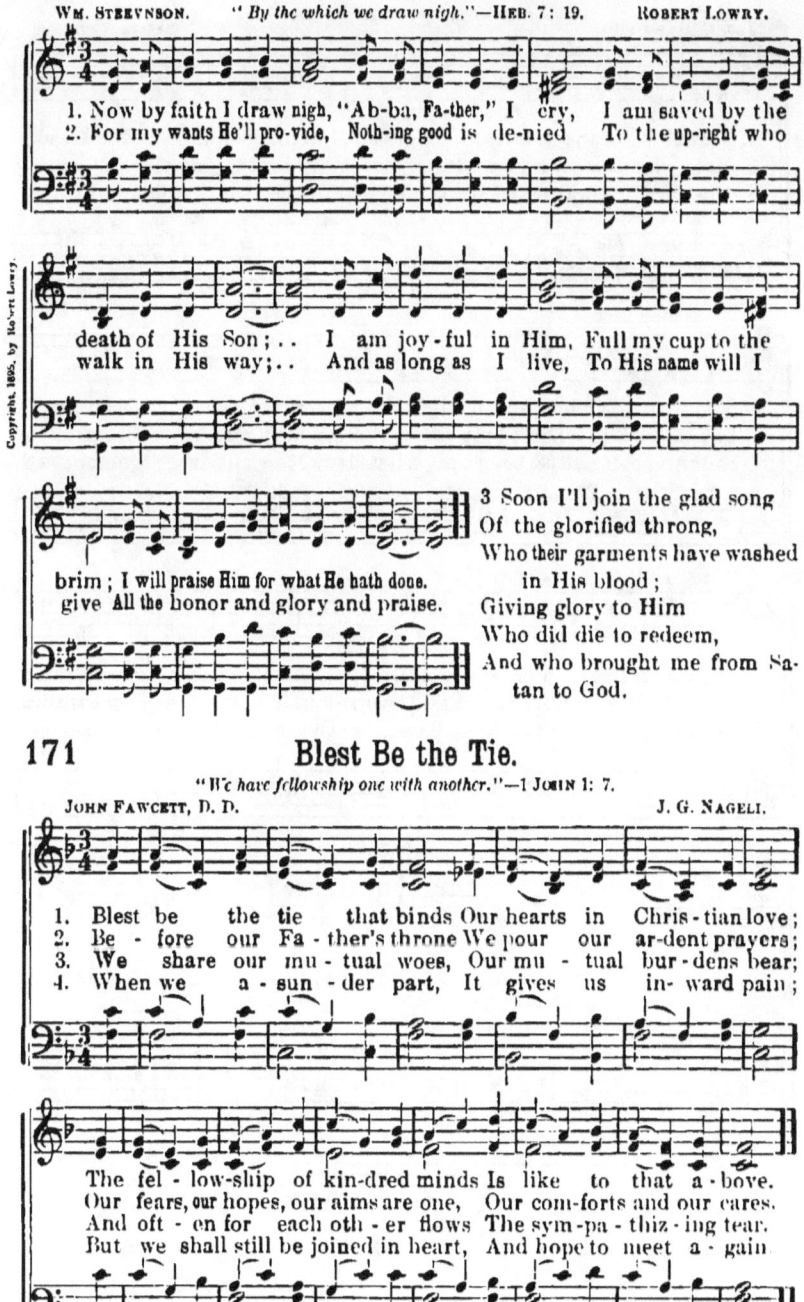

1. Now by faith I draw nigh, "Ab-ba, Fa-ther," I cry, I am saved by the death of His Son;.. I am joy-ful in Him, Full my cup to the brim; I will praise Him for what He hath done.
2. For my wants He'll pro-vide, Noth-ing good is de-nied To the up-right who walk in His way;.. And as long as I live, To His name will I give All the honor and glory and praise.
3. Soon I'll join the glad song
Of the glorified throng,
Who their garments have washed
in His blood;
Giving glory to Him
Who did die to redeem,
And who brought me from Sa-
tan to God.

171. Blest Be the Tie.

"We have fellowship one with another."—1 JOHN 1: 7.

JOHN FAWCETT, D. D. J. G. NAGELI.

1. Blest be the tie that binds Our hearts in Chris-tian love;
2. Be - fore our Fa - ther's throne We pour our ar-dent prayers;
3. We share our mu - tual woes, Our mu - tual bur - dens bear;
4. When we a - sun - der part, It gives us in - ward pain;

The fel - low-ship of kin-dred minds Is like to that a - bove.
Our fears, our hopes, our aims are one, Our com-forts and our cares.
And oft - en for each oth - er flows The sym-pa - thiz - ing tear.
But we shall still be joined in heart, And hope to meet a - gain.

We Praise Thee, O God. Concluded.

REFRAIN.

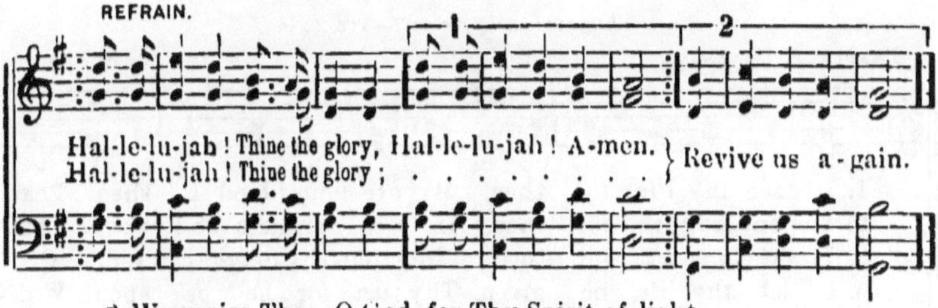

Hal-le-lu-jah! Thine the glory, Hal-le-lu-jah! A-men.
Hal-le-lu-jah! Thine the glory; . . . . } Revive us a-gain.

2 We praise Thee, O God, for Thy Spirit of light,
Who has shown us our Saviour, and scattered our night.

3 All glory and praise to the Lamb that was slain,
Who has borne all our sins, and has cleansed ev'ry stain.

4 All glory and praise to the God of all grace,
Who has bought us, and sought us, and guide our ways.

176   Jesus Bids You Draw Nigh.

"Made nigh by the blood of Christ."—EPH. 2: 13.

WM. STEVENSON.   ROBERT LOWRY.

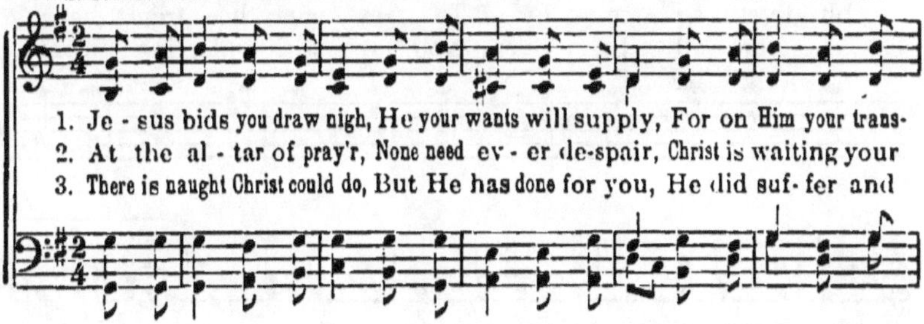

1. Je-sus bids you draw nigh, He your wants will supply, For on Him your trans-
2. At the al-tar of pray'r, None need ev-er de-spair, Christ is waiting your
3. There is naught Christ could do, But He has done for you, He did suf-fer and

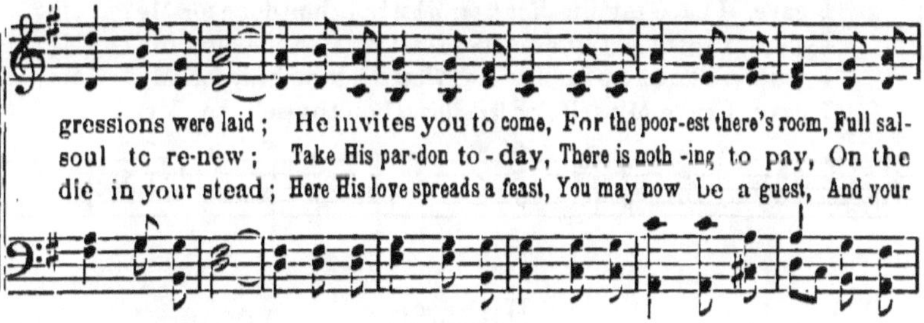

gressions were laid; He invites you to come, For the poor-est there's room, Full sal-
soul to re-new; Take His par-don to-day, There is noth-ing to pay, On the
die in your stead; Here His love spreads a feast, You may now be a guest, And your

va-tion for all He has made.
cross it was purchased for you.
soul from His boun-ty be fed.

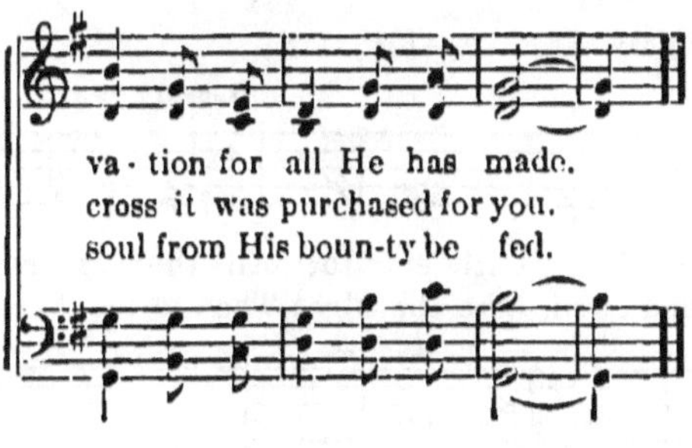

4 He is knocking once more;
Will you open the door?
In your heart He will set up His throne;
He will cleanse you from sin
If you now let Him in,
And as King He will reign there alone.

177. What Hast Thou done for Me?

"Who gave himself for us."—TIT. 2: 14.

FRANCES R. HAVERGAL.   W. D. HOWARD.

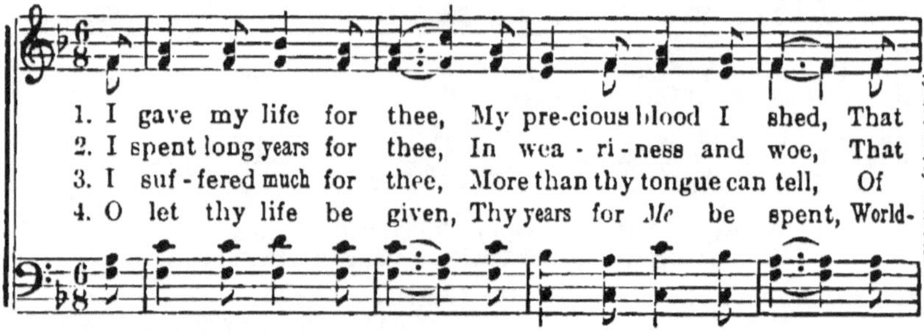

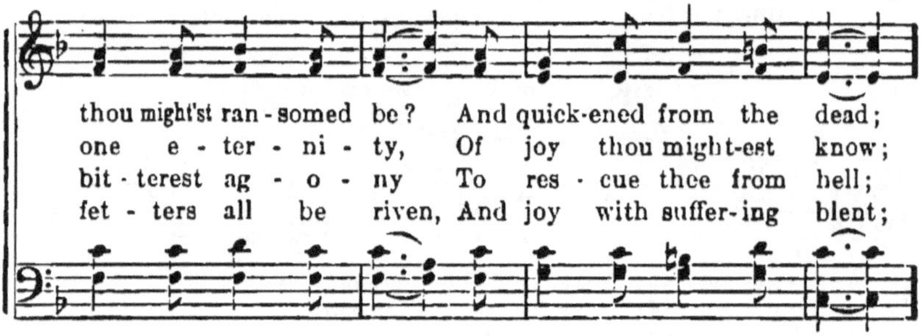

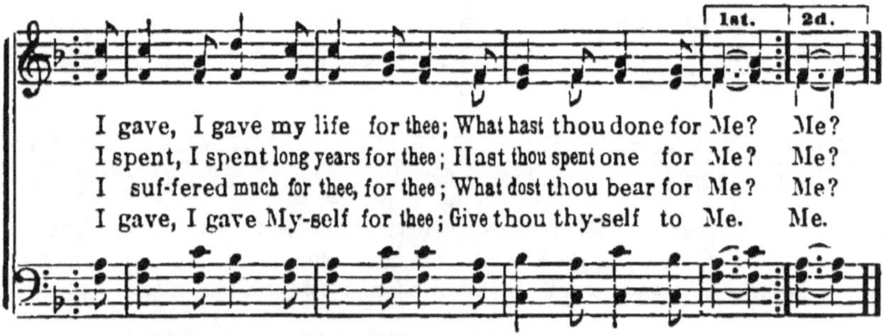

1. I gave my life for thee, My precious blood I shed, That thou might'st ransomed be? And quickened from the dead; I gave, I gave my life for thee; What hast thou done for Me? Me?
2. I spent long years for thee, In weariness and woe, That one eternity, Of joy thou might-est know; I spent, I spent long years for thee; Hast thou spent one for Me? Me?
3. I suffered much for thee, More than thy tongue can tell, Of bitterest agony To rescue thee from hell; I suffered much for thee, for thee; What dost thou bear for Me? Me?
4. O let thy life be given, Thy years for Me be spent, World-fetters all be riven, And joy with suffering blent; I gave, I gave Myself for thee; Give thou thyself to Me. Me.

178. Hitherto.

"Hitherto hath the LORD helped us."—1 SAM. 7: 12.

ANNIE S. HAWKS.   ROBERT LOWRY.

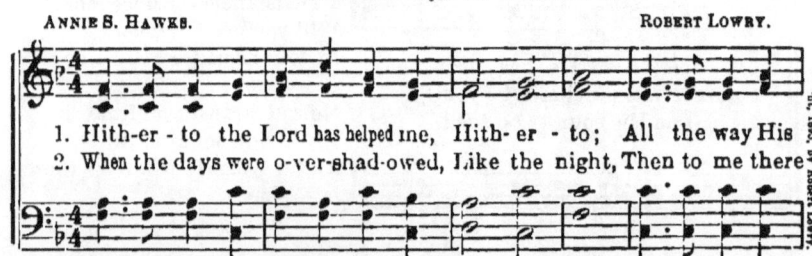

1. Hitherto the Lord has helped me, Hitherto; All the way His
2. When the days were overshadowed, Like the night, Then to me there

182. While Jesus Whispers.

"*Come unto me.*" — MATT. 11: 28.

WILL. E. WITTER. H. R. PALMER.

1. While Jesus whispers to you, Come, sinner, come!
   While we are praying for you, Come, sinner, come!
   Now is the time to own Him, Come, sinner, come!
   Now is the time to know Him, Come, sinner, come!

2. Are you too heavy laden?
   Come, sinner, come!
   Jesus will bear your burden,
   Come, sinner, come!
   Jesus will not deceive you,
   Come, sinner, come!
   Jesus can now redeem you,
   Come, sinner, come!

3. Oh, hear His tender pleading,
   Come, sinner, come!
   Come and receive His blessing,
   Come, sinner, come!
   While Jesus whispers to you,
   Come, sinner, come!
   While we are praying for you,
   Come, sinner, come!

183. Just as I Am.

"*We have redemption through his blood.*" — EPH. 1: 7.

CHARLOTTE ELLIOTT. WM. B. BRADBURY, by per.

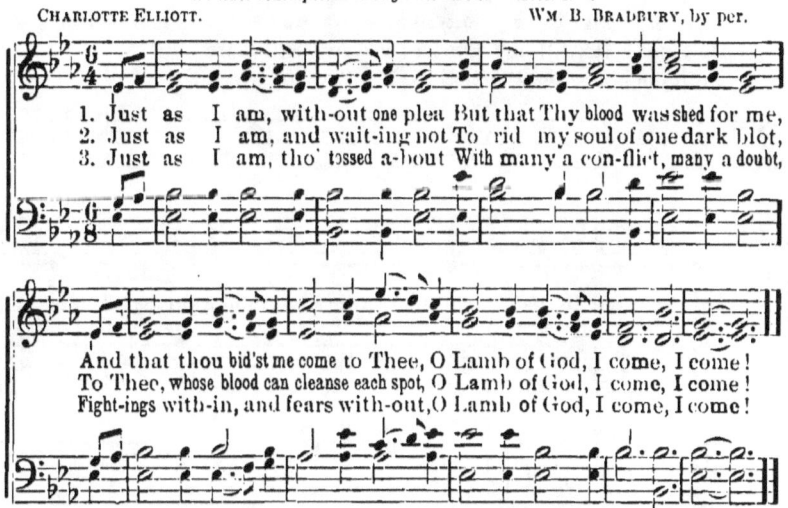

1. Just as I am, without one plea But that Thy blood was shed for me,
2. Just as I am, and waiting not To rid my soul of one dark blot,
3. Just as I am, tho' tossed about With many a conflict, many a doubt,

And that thou bid'st me come to Thee, O Lamb of God, I come, I come!
To Thee, whose blood can cleanse each spot, O Lamb of God, I come, I come!
Fightings within, and fears without, O Lamb of God, I come, I come!

4. Just as I am,—Thou wilt receive,
   Wilt welcome, pardon, cleanse, relieve;
   Because Thy promise I believe,
   O Lamb of God, I come, I come!

5. Just as I am,—Thy love unknown
   Has broken every barrier down;
   Now, to be Thine, yea, Thine alone
   O Lamb of God, I come, I come!

184. I Must Tell Jesus.

"Went and told Jesus.." —MATT. 14: 12.

E. A. H.
REV. ELISHA A. HOFFMAN.

1. I must tell Jesus all of my tri-als, I can-not bear these bur-dens a-lone; In my dis-tress He kind-ly will help me, He ev-er loves and cares for His own.

2. I must tell Jesus all of my troub-les; He is a kind, com-pas-sion-ate Friend; If I but ask Him, He will de-liv-er, Make of my troub-les quick-ly an end.

3. Tempt-ed and tried I need a great Sav-iour, One who can help my bur-dens to bear; I must tell Je-sus, I must tell Je-sus; He all my care and sor-rows will share.

4. O how the world to e-vil al-lures me! O how my heart is tempt-ed to sin! I must tell Je-sus, and He will help me O-ver the world the vic-t'ry to win.

CHORUS.

I must tell Je-sus! I must tell Je-sus! I can-not bear my bur-dens a-lone; I must tell Je-sus, I must tell Je-sus, Je-sus can help me, Je-sus a-lone.

185. Will Jesus Find Us Watching?

"Blessed are those servants whom the Lord, when he cometh, shall find watching."
LUKE 12: 37.

FANNY J. CROSBY.   W. H. DOANE.

1. When Jesus comes to reward His servants, Whether it be noon or night, Faithful to Him, will He find us watching, With our lamps all trimmed and bright?

2. If at the dawn of the early morning, He shall call us one by one, When to the Lord we restore our talents, Will He answer thee, "Well done"?

3. Have we been true to the trust He left us? Do we seek to do our best? If in our hearts there is naught condemns us, We shall have a glorious rest.

4. Blessed are those whom the Lord finds watching; In His glory they shall share; If He shall come at the dawn or midnight, Will He find us watching there?

REFRAIN.

Oh, can we say we are ready, brother? Ready for the soul's bright home? Say, will He find you and me still watching, Waiting, waiting when the Lord shall come?

190. I Bless the Lord.

"Sing unto the Lord, bless his name." — Ps. 96. 2.

Fanny J. Crosby. W. H. Doane.

1. I bless the Lord whose faithful hand Has led me all my days,
2. I bless the Lord whose tender care Is o'er me day by day;
3. In pleasant vales He guides my feet, Where rose and lily grow,
4. I bless the Lord whose wondrous love Prepares a home for me;

Who fills my soul with holy joy, My tongue with sweetest praise.
Who gently chides my wayward heart, And takes my sins away.
Then bids me rest beneath the shade, Where brook and fountain flow.
A glorious home not made with hands, Beyond the narrow sea.

REFRAIN.

I will sing, .. I will sing, .. A song to Him my heart shall raise,
I will sing,   I will sing,

Who fills my soul with holy joy, My tongue with sacred praise.

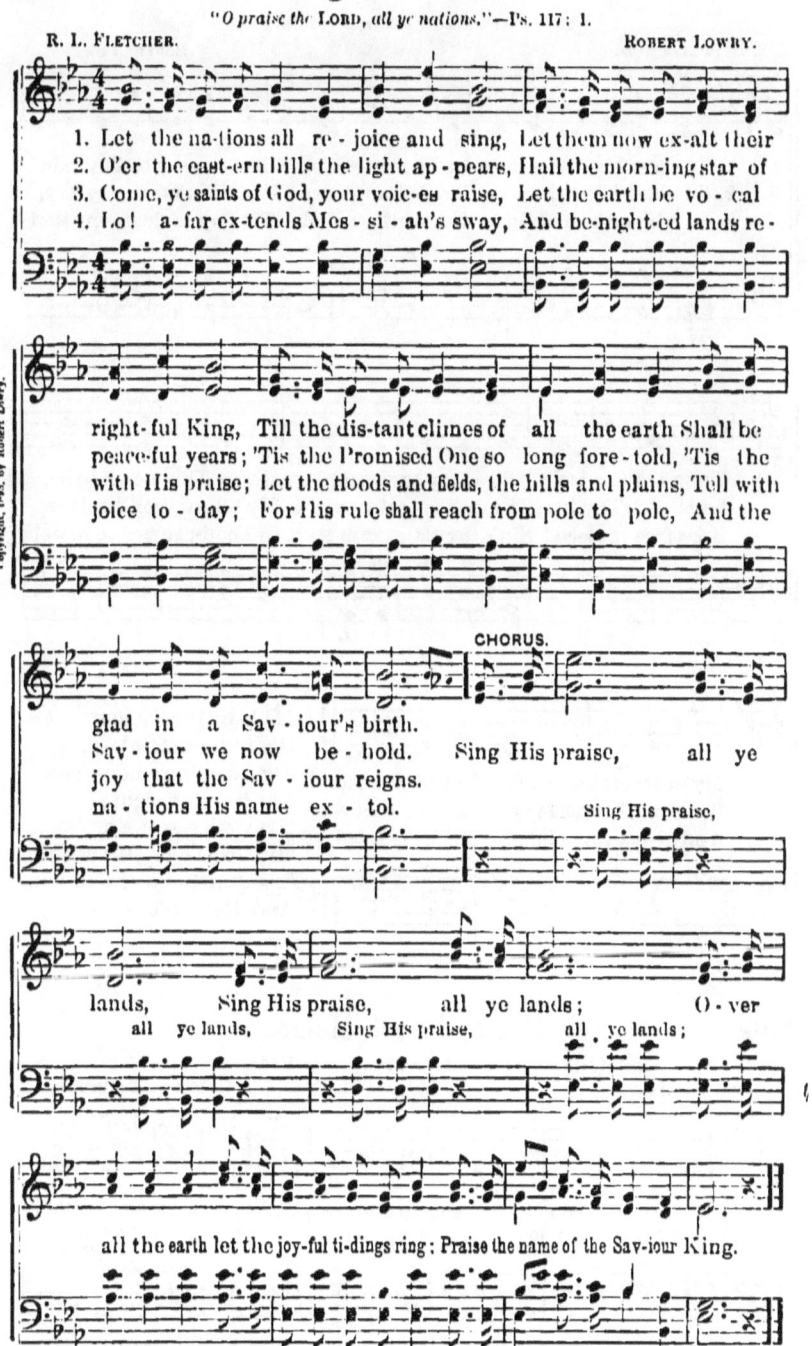

193. Jesus, I Would Abide.

"The truth shall make you free."—JOHN 8: 32.

S. D. PHELPS, D.D. ROBERT LOWRY.

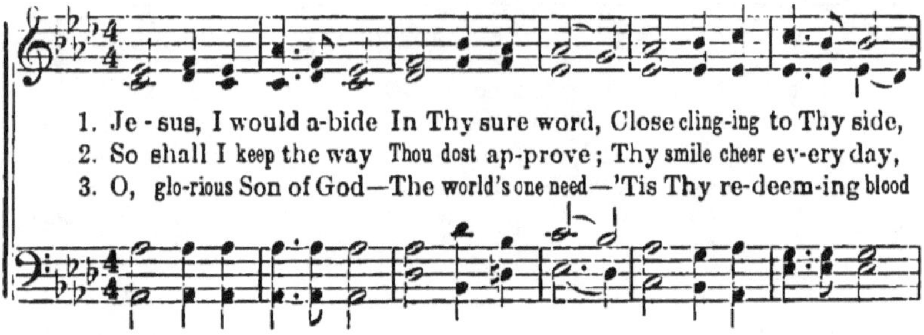

1. Je-sus, I would a-bide In Thy sure word, Close cling-ing to Thy side,
2. So shall I keep the way Thou dost ap-prove; Thy smile cheer ev-ery day,
3. O, glo-rious Son of God—The world's one need—'Tis Thy re-deem-ing blood

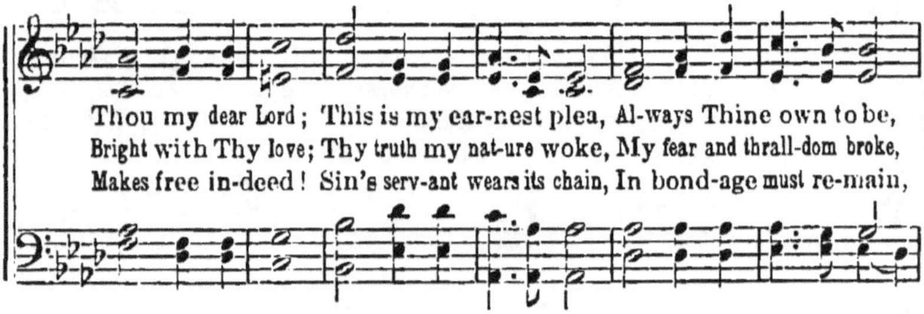

Thou my dear Lord; This is my ear-nest plea, Al-ways Thine own to be,
Bright with Thy love; Thy truth my nat-ure woke, My fear and thrall-dom broke,
Makes free in-deed! Sin's serv-ant wears its chain, In bond-age must re-main,

My heart and life with Thee In full ac-cord.
Bro't me, be-neath Thy yoke, Rest from a-bove.
And ev-ery hope be vain Till he is freed.

4 Made by the Saviour free—
Oh, blessed state!—
Then death we never see,
Nor feel its weight;
'Tis vict'ry over sin,
'Tis God's own peace within,
'Tis Christ Himself to win,
And Heaven's estate!

Copyright, 1886, by Robert Lowry.

194. Home, Sweet Home.

"A better country, that is an heavenly."—HEB. 11: 16.

DAVID DENHAM. HENRY R. BISHOP.

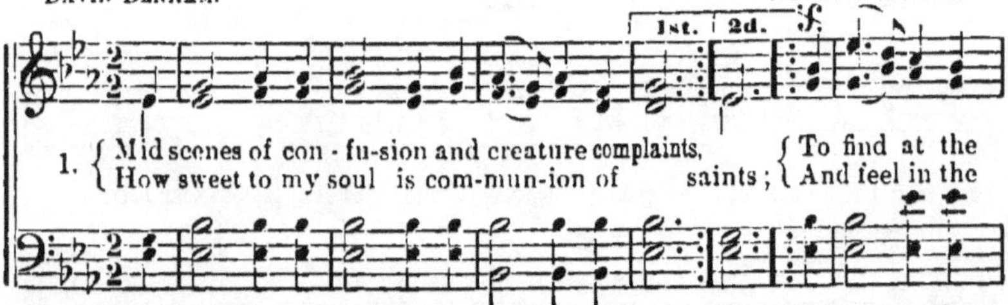

1. { Mid scenes of con-fu-sion and creature complaints, { To find at the
   { How sweet to my soul is com-mun-ion of saints; { And feel in the

D. S. *Prepare me, dear*

Home, Sweet Home. Concluded.

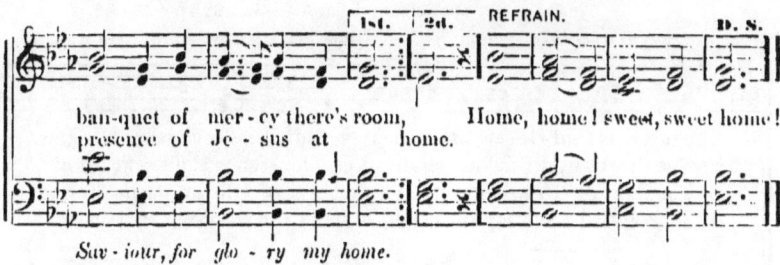

1st.
2d.
REFRAIN.
D. S.
ban-quet of mer - cy there's room, Home, home! sweet, sweet home!
presence of Je - sus at home.
Sav - iour, for glo - ry my home.

2 Sweet bonds that unite all the children of peace!
And thrice precious Jesus, whose love cannot cease!
Though oft from Thy presence in sadness I roam,
I long to behold Thee in glory at home.

3 While here in the valley of conflict I stay,
O give me submission, and strength as my day;
In all my afflictions to Thee I would come,
Rejoicing in hope of my glorious home.

195 Near the Cross.

—"*peace through the blood of his cross.*"—Col. 1: 20.

Fanny J. Crosby. W. H. Doane.

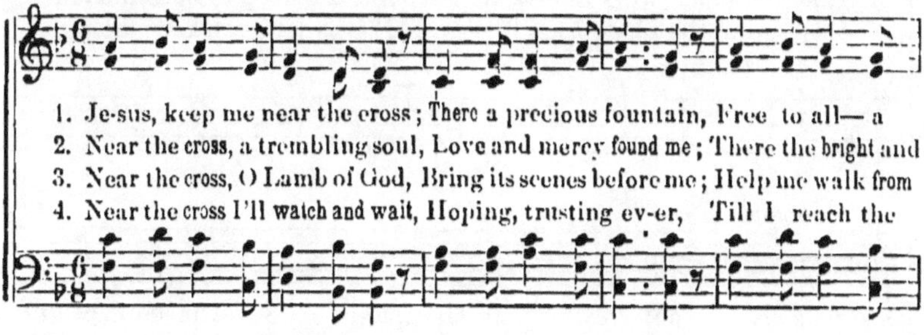
1. Je-sus, keep me near the cross; There a precious fountain, Free to all— a
2. Near the cross, a trembling soul, Love and mercy found me; There the bright and
3. Near the cross, O Lamb of God, Bring its scenes before me; Help me walk from
4. Near the cross I'll watch and wait, Hoping, trusting ev-er, Till I reach the

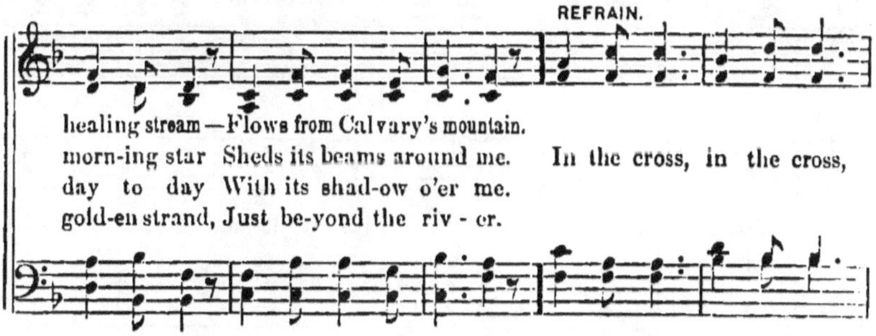
REFRAIN.
healing stream—Flows from Calvary's mountain.
morn-ing star Sheds its beams around me. In the cross, in the cross,
day to day With its shad-ow o'er me.
gold-en strand, Just be-yond the riv - er.

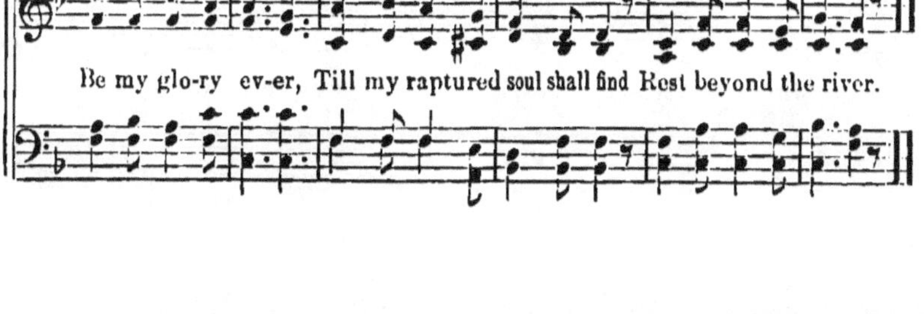
Be my glo-ry ev-er, Till my raptured soul shall find Rest beyond the river.

197. On Christ, the Solid Rock.

"He shall set me up upon a rock." — Ps. 27: 5.

EDWARD MOTE.   W. H. DOANE.

1. My hope is built on noth-ing less Than Je-sus' blood and right-eous-ness; I dare not trust the sweet-est frame, But whol-ly lean on Je-sus' name.
2. When dark-ness veils His love-ly face, I rest on His un-chang-ing grace; In ev-'ry high and storm-y gale, My an-chor holds with-in the veil.
3. His oath, His cov-e-nant and blood, Sup-port me in the whelm-ing flood; When all a-round my soul gives way, He then is all my hope and stay.

REFRAIN.

On Christ, the Sol-id Rock, I stand, All oth-er ground is sink-ing sand;

On Christ, the Sol-id Rock, I stand, All oth-er ground is sink-ing sand.

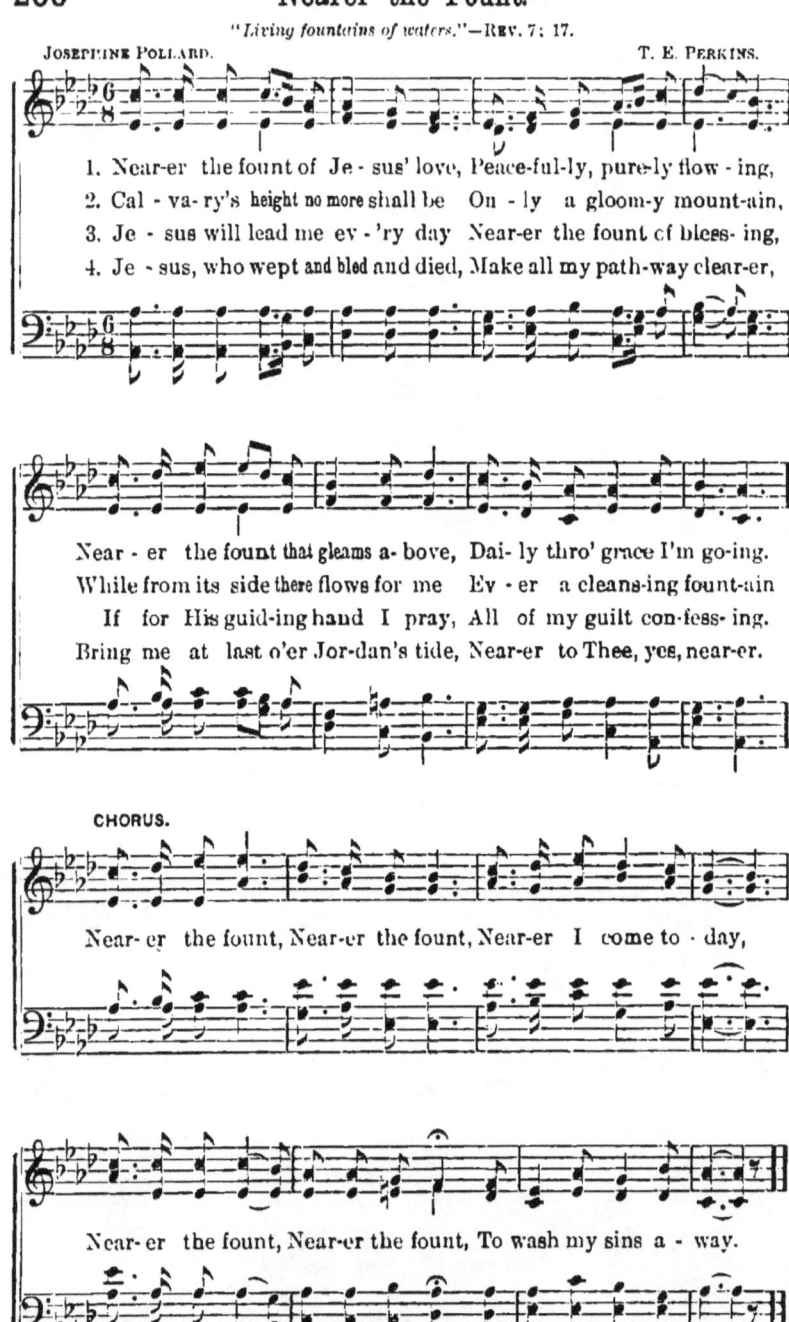

200 Nearer the Fount.

"Living fountains of waters."—REV. 7: 17.

JOSEPHINE POLLARD. T. E. PERKINS.

1. Near-er the fount of Je-sus' love, Peace-ful-ly, pure-ly flow-ing,
2. Cal-va-ry's height no more shall be On-ly a gloom-y mount-ain,
3. Je-sus will lead me ev-'ry day Near-er the fount of bless-ing,
4. Je-sus, who wept and bled and died, Make all my path-way clear-er,

Near-er the fount that gleams a-bove, Dai-ly thro' grace I'm go-ing.
While from its side there flows for me Ev-er a cleans-ing fount-ain
If for His guid-ing hand I pray, All of my guilt con-fess-ing.
Bring me at last o'er Jor-dan's tide, Near-er to Thee, yes, near-er.

CHORUS.

Near-er the fount, Near-er the fount, Near-er I come to-day,

Near-er the fount, Near-er the fount, To wash my sins a-way.

Copyright, 1890, by W. B. Pearce.

The Bolted Door. Concluded.

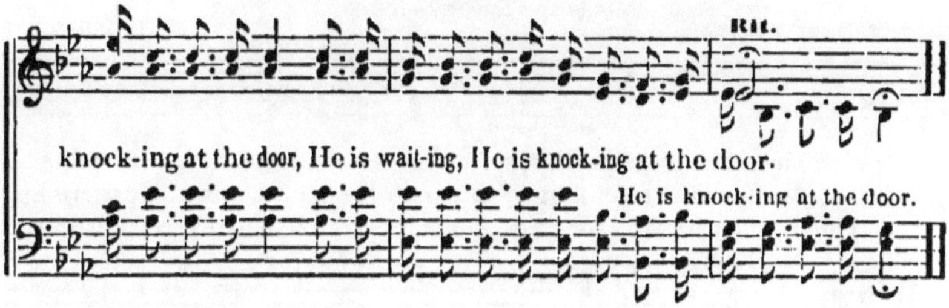

knock-ing at the door, He is wait-ing, He is knock-ing at the door. He is knock-ing at the door.

---

203. Give Thy Heart To Me.

"Give me thine heart."—Prov. 23: 26.

FANNY J. CROSBY.　　　　　　　　　　　　　　W. H. DOANE.
SOLO.

1. Hark! there comes a whis-per Steal-ing on thine ear; 'Tis the Sav-iour call-ing, Soft, soft and clear.
2. With that voice so gen-tle, Dost thou hear Him say, Tell me all thy sor-rows, Come, come a-way?
3. Wouldst thou find a ref-uge For thy soul op-pressed? Je-sus kind-ly an-swers, I am thy rest.
4. At the cross of Je-sus Let thy bur-den fall, While He gen-tly whis-pers, I'll bear it all.

REFRAIN.

Give thy heart to me, Once I died for thee; Hark! hark! thy Sav-iour calls, Come, sin-ner, come.

Just now, O come,

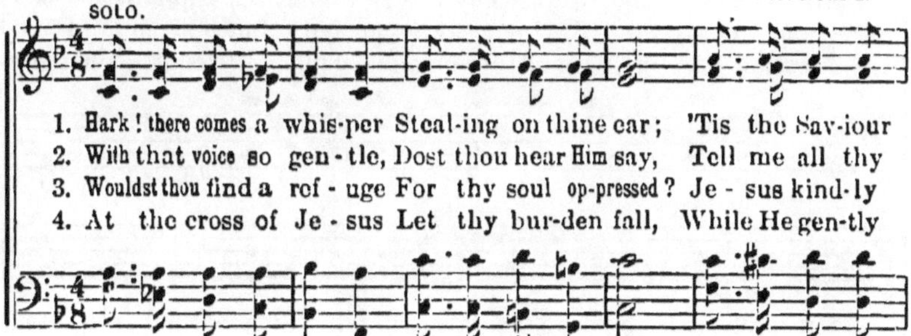

Fling Out the Banner. Concluded.

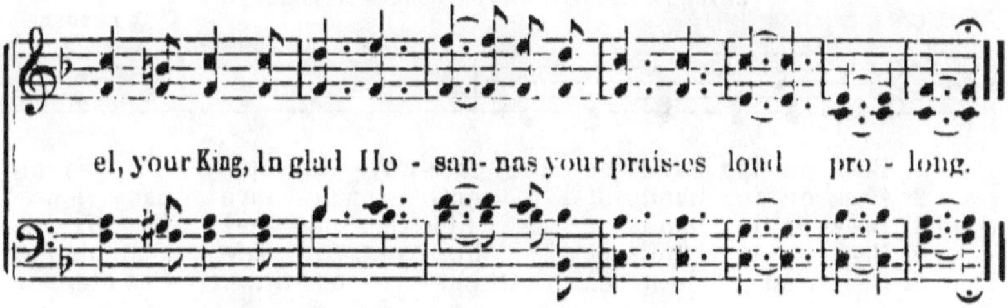

el, your King, In glad Ho - san - nas your prais-es loud pro - long.

205 In Exile Here We Wander.

"Here have we no continuing city."—HEB. 13: 14.

WILLIAM COOKE. ROBERT LOWRY.

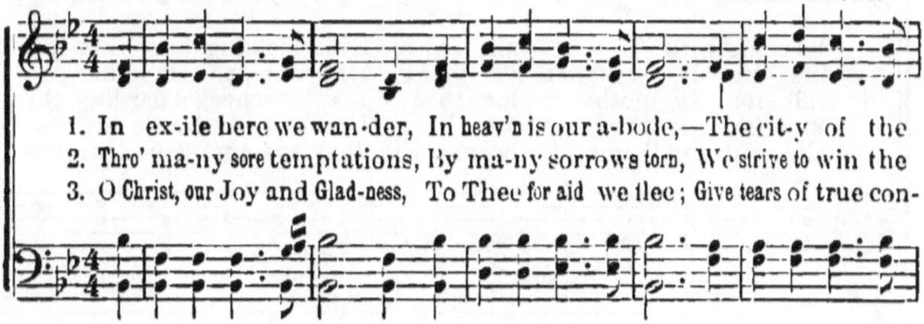

1. In ex-ile here we wan-der, In heav'n is our a-bode,—The cit-y of the
2. Thro' ma-ny sore temptations, By ma-ny sorrows torn, We strive to win the
3. O Christ, our Joy and Glad-ness, To Thee for aid we flee; Give tears of true con-

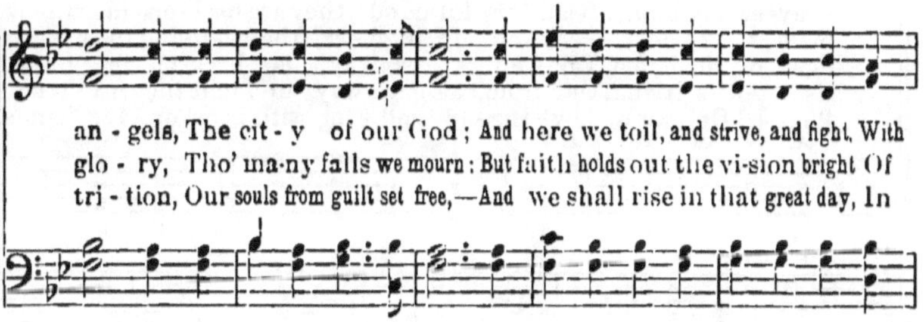

an - gels, The cit - y of our God; And here we toil, and strive, and fight, With
glo - ry, Tho' ma-ny falls we mourn: But faith holds out the vi-sion bright Of
tri - tion, Our souls from guilt set free,—And we shall rise in that great day, In

sin and woe op-pressed; There God will give the sons of light E - ter-nal joy and rest.
our e-ter-nal home; And hope as-sures that realm of light, When we have o-ver-come.
bod-ies like to Thine, And with Thy saints, in bright ar-ray, Shall in Thy glo-ry shine.

Copyright, 1891, by Robert Lowry.

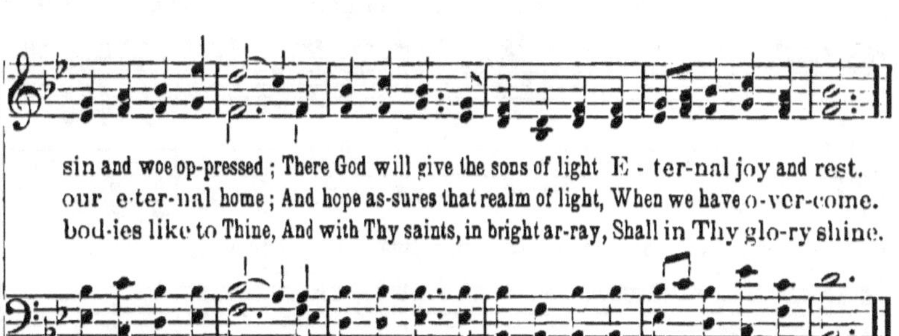

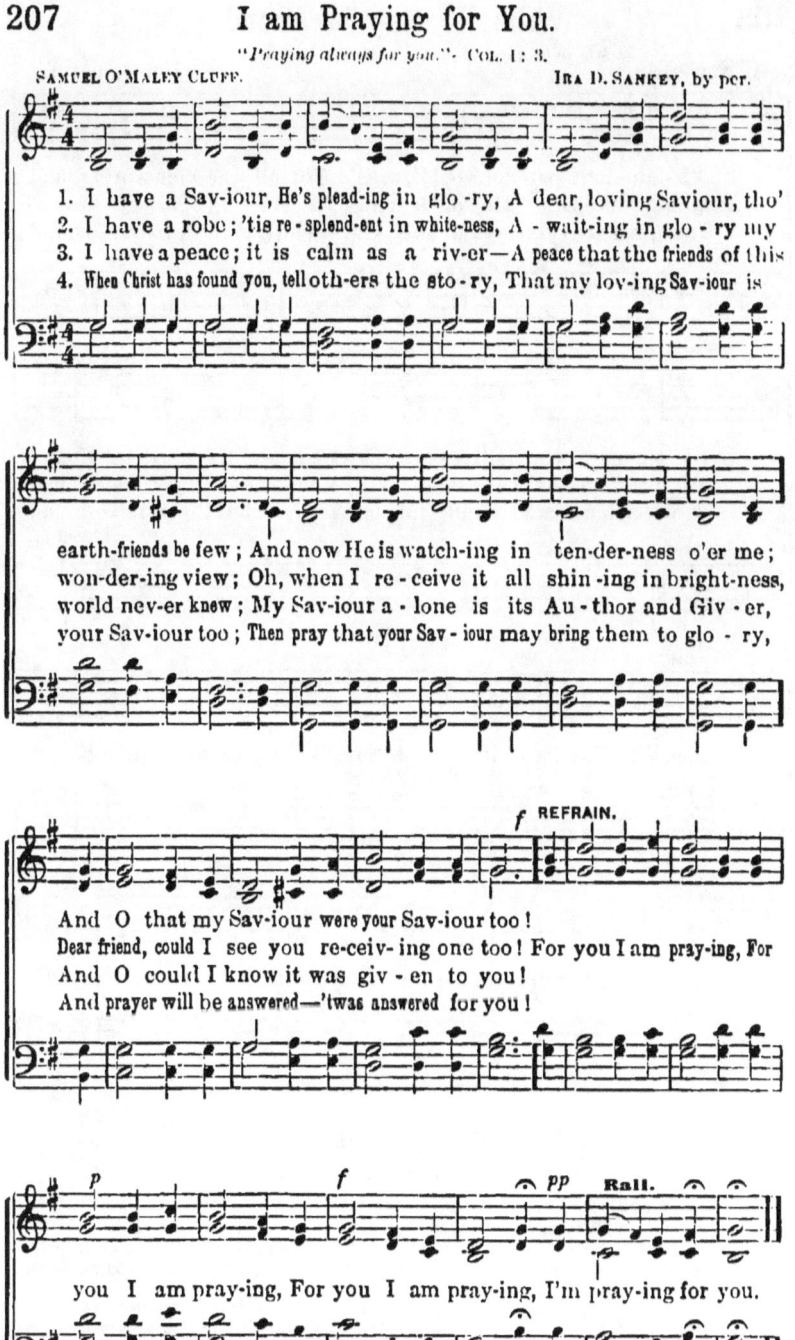

208. While He May be Found.

"Seek ye the Lord while he may be found." —Isa. 55: 6.

D. W. Whittle — W. H. Doane

1. A-bun-dant par-don God hath said, For all the wide world round
Of sinners who shall seek His face While now He may be found.
2. Think what it is He of-fers thee, To be in glo-ry crown'd,
To live with Christ e-ter-nal-ly, Where nought but joy is found.
3. Tho' great your sins, yet great-er still Shall grace in Christ a-bound;
What God hath said He will ful-fill; Then seek till you have found.

CHORUS.
Then seek the Lord with-out de-lay, While grace may yet a-bound;
O come with thy sins, and seek Him to-day, O Come while He may be found.

Copyright, 1896, by W. H. Doane.

209. O Thou, my Soul. L. M.

"In thee is my trust." —Ps. 141: 8.

1 O thou, my soul, forget no more
The Friend who all thy sorrows bore;
Let every idol be forgot;
But, O my soul, forget Him not.

2 Renounce thy works and ways with grief,
And fly to this divine relief;
Nor Him forget who left His throne,
And for thy life gave up His own.

3 Eternal truth and mercy shine
In Him, and He Himself is thine;
And canst thou, then, with sin beset,
Such charms, such matchless charms, forget?

4 Oh, no; till life itself depart,
His name shall cheer and warm my heart;
And, lisping this, from earth I'll rise,
And join the chorus of the skies.

Krishnu Pal.

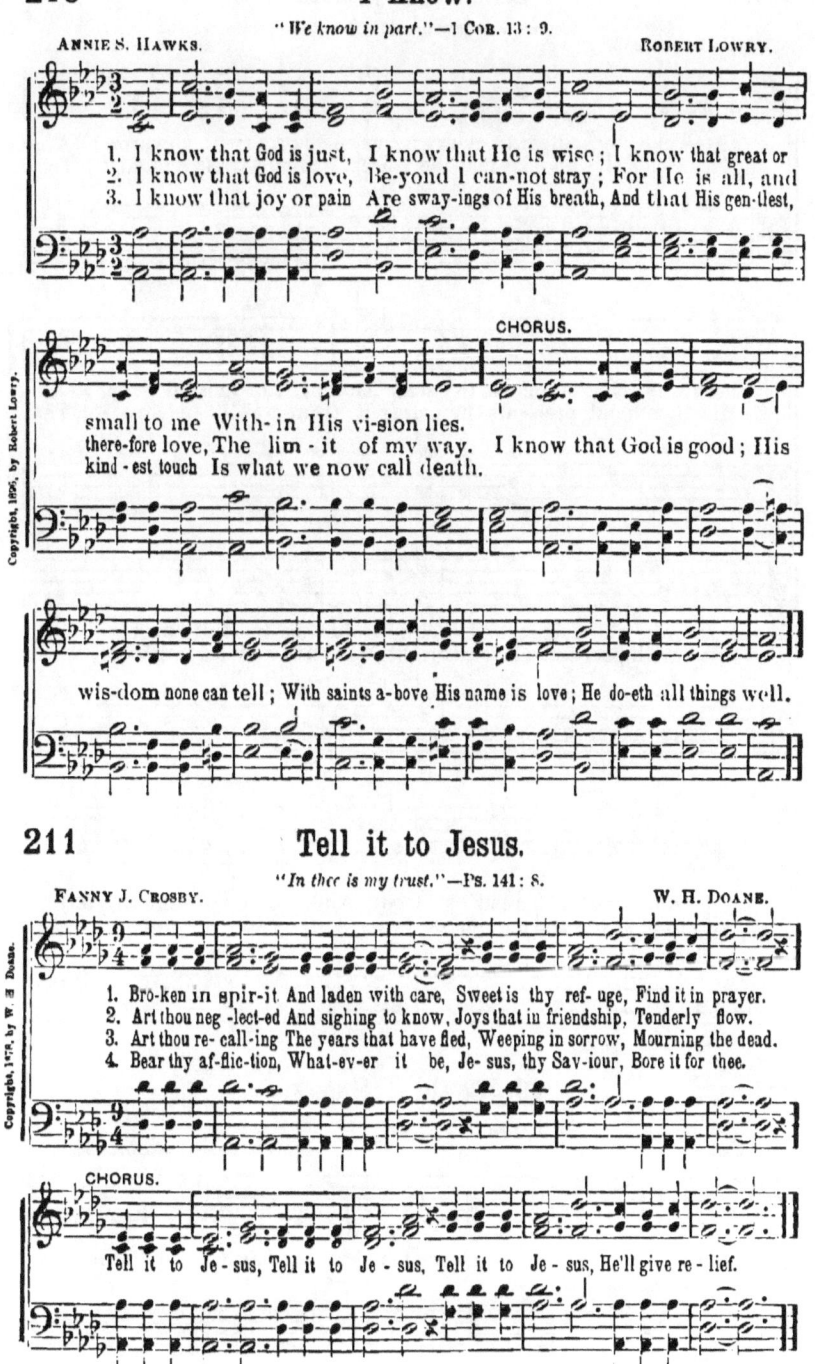

212. Awake, My Soul.

"So run, that ye may obtain."—1 Cor. 9: 24.

PHILIP DODDRIDGE.   ROBERT LOWRY.

1. A-wake, my soul, stretch ev-ery nerve, And press with vig-or on; A heav'n-ly race de-mands thy zeal, And an im-mor-tal crown.
2. A cloud of wit-ness-es a-round Hold thee in full sur-vey; For-get the steps al-read-y trod, And on-ward urge thy way.
3. 'Tis God's all-an-i-mat-ing voice That calls thee from on high; 'Tis His own hand pre-sents the prize To thine up-lift-ed eye;—
4. That prize, with peer-less glo-ries bright, Which shall new lus-tre boast, When vic-tors' wreaths and mon-archs' gems Shall blend in com-mon dust.

213. Oh, Could I Speak.

"Worthy is the Lamb."—Rev. 5: 12.

S. MEDLEY.   DR. LOWELL MASON. Arr.

1. Oh, could I speak the match-less worth, Oh, could I sound the

Oh, Could I Speak. Concluded.

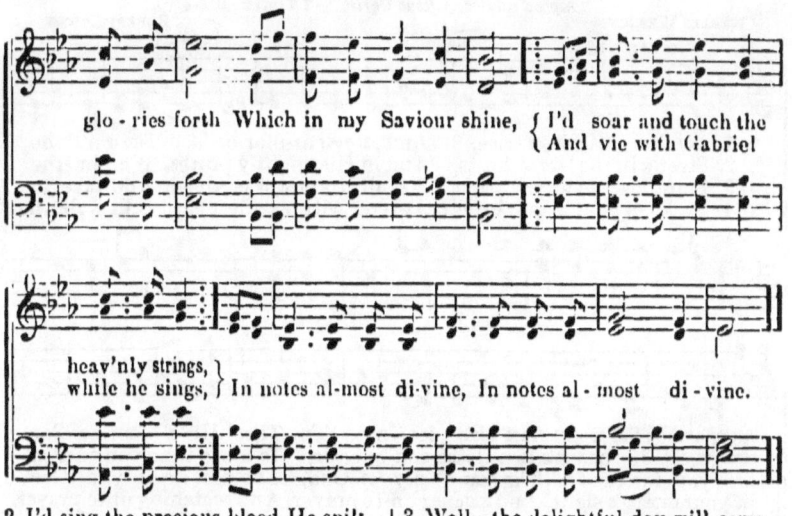

glo-ries forth Which in my Saviour shine, { I'd soar and touch the heav'nly strings,
And vie with Gabriel while he sings, } In notes al-most di-vine, In notes al-most di-vine.

2 I'd sing the precious blood He spilt,
My ransom from the dreadful guilt
Of sin, and wrath divine;
I'd sing His glorious righteousness,
In which all perfect heavenly dress
‖:My soul shall ever shine.:‖

3 Well—the delightful day will come,
When my dear Lord will bring me home,
And I shall see His face;
Then with my Saviour, Brother, Friend,
A blest eternity I'll spend,
‖:Triumphant in His grace.:‖

214 Must Jesus Bear the Cross?

"*Ye are partakers of Christ's sufferings.*"—1 PET. 4: 13.

THOS. SHEPHERD.   GEORGE N. ALLEN.

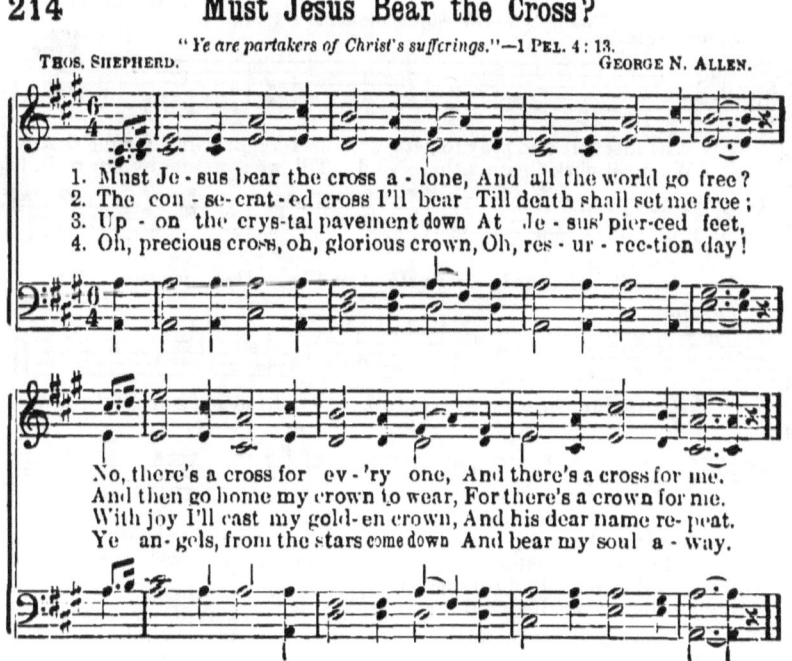

1. Must Je-sus bear the cross a-lone, And all the world go free?
2. The con-se-crat-ed cross I'll bear Till death shall set me free;
3. Up-on the crys-tal pavement down At Je-sus' pier-ced feet,
4. Oh, precious cross, oh, glorious crown, Oh, res-ur-rec-tion day!

No, there's a cross for ev-'ry one, And there's a cross for me.
And then go home my crown to wear, For there's a crown for me.
With joy I'll cast my gold-en crown, And his dear name re-peat.
Ye an-gels, from the stars come down And bear my soul a-way.

215. Soldiers of Christ, Arise.

"A good soldier of Jesus Christ."—2 Tim. 2: 3.

CHARLES WESLEY.　　　　　　　　　　　　　　　　ROBERT LOWRY.

With vigor.

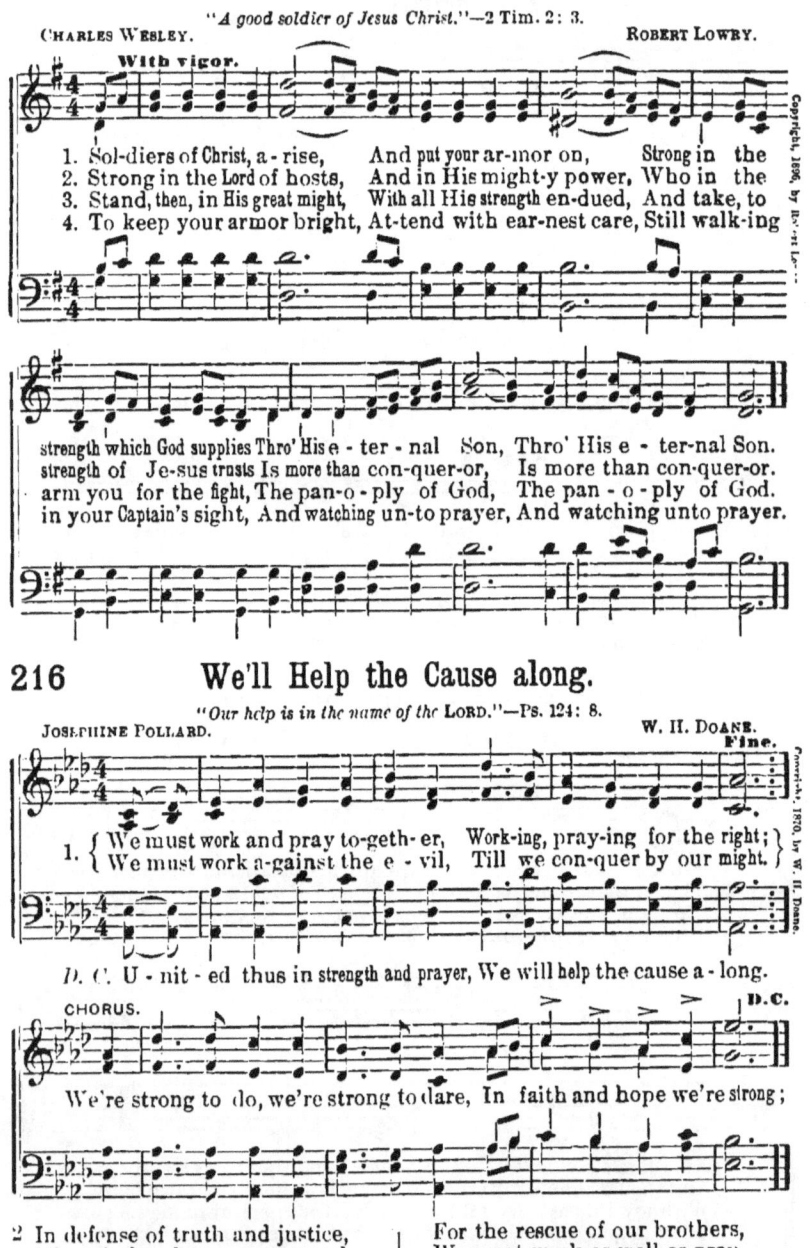

1. Sol-diers of Christ, a-rise, And put your ar-mor on, Strong in the strength which God supplies Thro' His e-ter-nal Son, Thro' His e-ter-nal Son.
2. Strong in the Lord of hosts, And in His might-y power, Who in the strength of Je-sus trusts Is more than con-quer-or, Is more than con-quer-or.
3. Stand, then, in His great might, With all His strength en-dued, And take, to arm you for the fight, The pan-o-ply of God, The pan-o-ply of God.
4. To keep your armor bright, At-tend with ear-nest care, Still walk-ing in your Captain's sight, And watching un-to prayer, And watching unto prayer.

216. We'll Help the Cause along.

"Our help is in the name of the LORD."—Ps. 124: 8.

JOSEPHINE POLLARD.　　　　　　　　　　　　　　　W. H. DOANE.

1. { We must work and pray to-geth-er, Work-ing, pray-ing for the right;
     We must work a-gainst the e-vil, Till we con-quer by our might. }

D. C. U-nit-ed thus in strength and prayer, We will help the cause a-long.

CHORUS.

We're strong to do, we're strong to dare, In faith and hope we're strong;

2 In defense of truth and justice,
   Like a bulwark we must stand,
   And the soul that's full of courage
   Will give courage to the hand.

3 We must work and not be weary,
   Though we conquer not to-day;
   For the rescue of our brothers,
   We must work as well as pray.

4 Hark! the crystal streams and fountains
   Swell the chorus of our song;
   And they seem to be rejoicing
   As they help the cause along.

217. Bringing in the Sheaves.

"The harvest is the end of the world."—Matt. 13: 39.

KNOWLES SHAW.   GEO. A. MINOR.

1. Sow-ing in the morn-ing, sow-ing seeds of kindness, Sow-ing in the noon-tide and the dew-y eves;
Wait-ing for the har-vest and the time of reap-ing, (*Omit*) } We shall come re-joic-ing, bring-ing in the sheaves.

CHORUS.

Bringing in the sheaves, bringing in the sheaves, We shall come rejoicing, bringing in the sheaves;

2 Sowing in the sunshine, sowing in the shadows,
   Fearing neither clouds nor winter's chilling breeze;
By and by the harvest, and the labor ended,
   We shall come rejoicing, bringing in the sheaves.

3 Go, then, ever weeping, sowing for the Master,
   Though the loss sustained our spirit often grieves;
When our weeping's over, He will bid us welcome,
   We shall come rejoicing, bringing in the sheaves.

218. Work, for the Night is Coming.

"The night cometh."—John 9: 4.

1 Work, for the night is coming,
   Work thro' the morning hours;
Work while the dew is sparkling,
   Work 'mid springing flowers:
Work when the day grows brighter,
   Work in the glowing sun;
Work, for the night is coming,
   When man's work is done.

2 Work, for the night is coming,
   Work thro' the sunny noon;
Fill brightest hours with labor,
   Rest comes sure and soon:
Give ev'ry flying minute
   Something to keep in store;
Work, for the night is coming,
   When man works no more.

3 Work, for the night is coming,
   Under the sunset skies;
While their bright tints are glowing,
   Work, for the daylight flies:
Work till the last beam fadeth,
   Fadeth to shine no more;
Work, while the night is darkening,
   When man's work is o'er.

ANNA L. WALKER.

219. We Shall Meet By and By.

"Then shall the righteous shine forth as the sun." — MATT. 13: 43.

JOHN ATKINSON, D.D. HUBERT P. MAIN.

1. We shall meet be-yond the riv-er,
   And the dark-ness will be o-ver, } By and by, by and by;
2. We shall strike the harps of glo-ry,
   We shall sing re-demp-tion's sto-ry, } By and by, by and by;
3. We shall see and be like Je-sus,
   Who a crown of life will give us, } By and by, by and by;

With the toil-some jour-ney done, And the glo-rious bat-tle won,
And the strains for ev-er-more Shall re-sound in sweet-ness o'er
And the an-gels who ful-fill All the man-dates of His will,

We shall shine forth as the sun, By and by, by and by.
Yon-der ev-er-last-ing shore, By and by, by and by.
Shall at-tend and love us still, By and by, by and by.

Copyright, 1880, by Hubert P. Main. Used by per.

220. How Firm a Foundation.

"Stand fast in the faith." — 1 COR. 16:13.

1 How firm a foundation, ye saints of the Lord,
Is laid for your faith in His excellent word!
What more can He say than to you He hath said,—
To you who for refuge to Jesus have fled?

2 " Fear not, I am with thee; O be not dismayed;
I, I am thy God, and will still give thee aid;
I'll strengthen thee, help thee, and cause thee to stand,
Upheld by my righteous, omnipotent hand.

3 " When through the deep waters I call thee to go,
The rivers of sorrow shall not overflow;
For I will be with thee, thy troubles to bless,
And sanctify to thee thy deepest distress.

4 " The soul that on Jesus hath leaned for repose
I will not, I will not desert to his foes;
That soul, though all hell should endeavor to shake,
I'll never, no, never, no, never forsake." GEORGE KEITH.

221. Take My Life, and Let it Be.

"Consecrate yourselves to-day to the Lord."—Exod. 32: 29.

FRANCES R. HAVERGAL.   W. D. HOWARD.

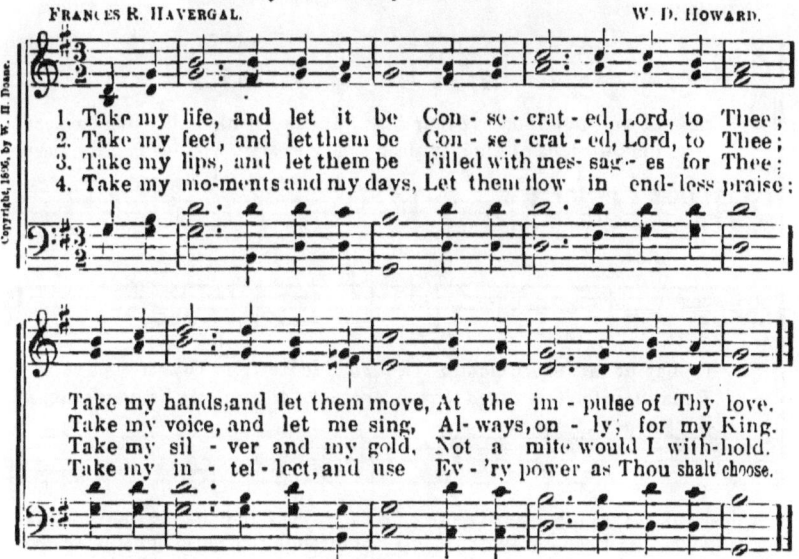

1. Take my life, and let it be Con-se-crat-ed, Lord, to Thee;
2. Take my feet, and let them be Con-se-crat-ed, Lord, to Thee;
3. Take my lips, and let them be Filled with mes-sag-es for Thee;
4. Take my mo-ments and my days, Let them flow in end-less praise:

Take my hands, and let them move, At the im-pulse of Thy love.
Take my voice, and let me sing, Al-ways, on-ly, for my King.
Take my sil-ver and my gold, Not a mite would I with-hold.
Take my in-tel-lect, and use Ev-'ry power as Thou shalt choose.

222. Jesus, Lover of My Soul.

"Thou art my refuge."—Ps. 142: 5.

REV. CHARLES WESLEY.   SIMEON B. MARSH.

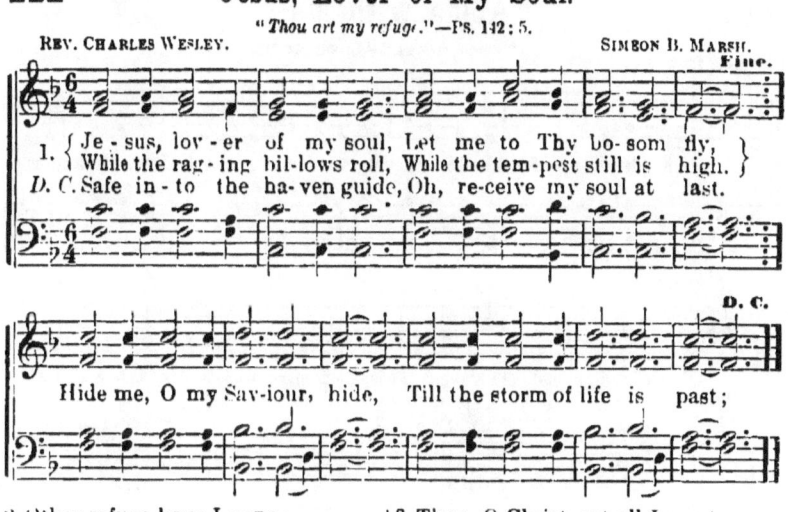

1. { Je-sus, lov-er of my soul, Let me to Thy bo-som fly, }
   { While the rag-ing bil-lows roll, While the tem-pest still is high. }
D.C. Safe in-to the ha-ven guide, Oh, re-ceive my soul at last.

Hide me, O my Sav-iour, hide, Till the storm of life is past;

2 Other refuge have I none;
  Hangs my helpless soul on Thee;
Leave, ah, leave me not alone,
  Still support and comfort me.
All my trust on Thee is stayed,
  All my help from Thee I bring;
Cover my defenseless head
  With the shadow of Thy wing.

3 Thou, O Christ, art all I want;
  All in all in Thee I find;
Raise the fallen, cheer the faint,
  Heal the sick, and lead the blind.
Just and holy is Thy name,
  I am all unrighteousness;
Vile and full of sin I am,
  Thou art full of truth and grace.

223. Sun of My Soul.

"Abide in me, and I in you." — JOHN 15: 4.

REV. JOHN KEBLE. PETER RITTER.

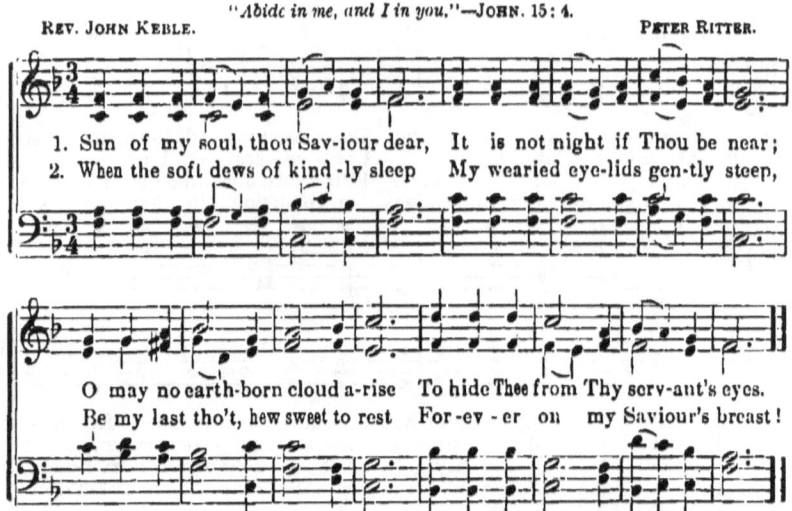

1. Sun of my soul, thou Saviour dear, It is not night if Thou be near; O may no earth-born cloud arise To hide Thee from Thy servant's eyes.
2. When the soft dews of kindly sleep My wearied eye-lids gently steep, Be my last tho't, how sweet to rest Forever on my Saviour's breast!

3 Abide with me from morn till eve,
For without Thee I can not live;
Abide with me when night is nigh,
For without Thee I dare not die.

4 Come near and bless us when we wake,
Ere through the world our way we take;
Till, in the ocean of Thy love,
We lose ourselves in heaven above.

224. Abide with Me.

"Abide with us." — LUKE 24: 29.

REV. H. F. LYTE. W. H. MONK.

1. Abide with me; fast falls the eventide; The darkness deepens—Lord, with me abide; When helpers fail, and other comforts flee, Help of the helpless, O abide with me!

2 Swift to its close ebbs out life's little day;
Earth's joys grow dim, its glories pass away
Change and decay in all around I see;
O Thou who changest not, abide with me!

3 Hold Thou Thy cross before my closing eyes;
Shine through the gloom, and point me to the skies;
Heaven's morning breaks, and earth's vain shadows flee;
In life, in death, O Lord, abide with me!

225. Softly Now the Light.

"Ye shall find rest unto your souls."—MATT. 11:29.

GEORGE W. DOANE. GEORGE HEWS.

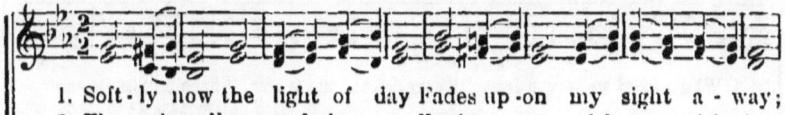

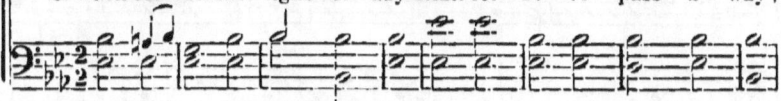

1. Soft-ly now the light of day Fades up-on my sight a-way;
2. Thou, whose all per-vad-ing eye Naught es-capes, with-out, with-in,
3. Soon for me the light of day Shall for-ev-er pass a-way;

Free from care, from lab-or—free, Lord, I would com-mune with Thee.
Par-don each in-firm-i-ty, O-pen fault, and se-cret sin.
Then from sin and sor-row free, Take me, Lord, to dwell with Thee.

226. O for a Closer Walk.

"Walk in the Spirit."—GAL. 5:16.

WILLIAM COWPER. DR. THOMAS HASTINGS.

1. O for a closer walk with God, A calm and heavenly frame, A light to shine up-
2. Return, O holy Dove, return, Sweet messenger of rest; I hate the sins that
3. The dearest idol I have known, What'er that i-dol be, Help me to tear it
4. So shall my walk be close with God, Calm and serene my frame; So purer light shall

on the road That leads me to the Lamb! That leads me to the Lamb!
made Thee mourn, And drove Thee from my breast, And drove Thee from my breast.
from Thy throne, And worship on-ly Thee, And wor-ship on-ly Thee.
mark the road That leads me to the Lamb, That leads me to the Lamb.

227. What a Friend.

"There is a friend that sticketh closer than a brother." —PROV. 18: 24.

JOSEPH SCRIVEN.   C. C. CONVERSE.

1. What a friend we have in Jesus, All our griefs and sins to bear! What a privilege to car-ry
D. S. All because we do not car-ry
Ev'rything to God in prayer! Oh, what peace we often forfeit, Oh, what needless pain we bear,
Ev'rything to God in prayer!

2 Have we trials and temptations?
   Is there trouble anywhere?
We should never be discouraged;
   Take it to the Lord in prayer;
Can we find a friend so faithful,
   Who will all our sorrows share?
Jesus knows our every weakness,
   Take it to the Lord in prayer.

3 Are we weak and heavy-laden,
   Cumbered with a load of care?
Precious Saviour, still our refuge,—
   Take it to the Lord in prayer;
Do thy friends despise, forsake thee?
   Take it to the Lord in prayer;
In His arms He'll take and shield thee,
   Thou wilt find a solace there.

228. Guide Me, Great Jehovah.

"The LORD shall guide thee continually." —ISA. 58: 11.

WILLIAM WILLIAMS.   DR. THOMAS HASTINGS.

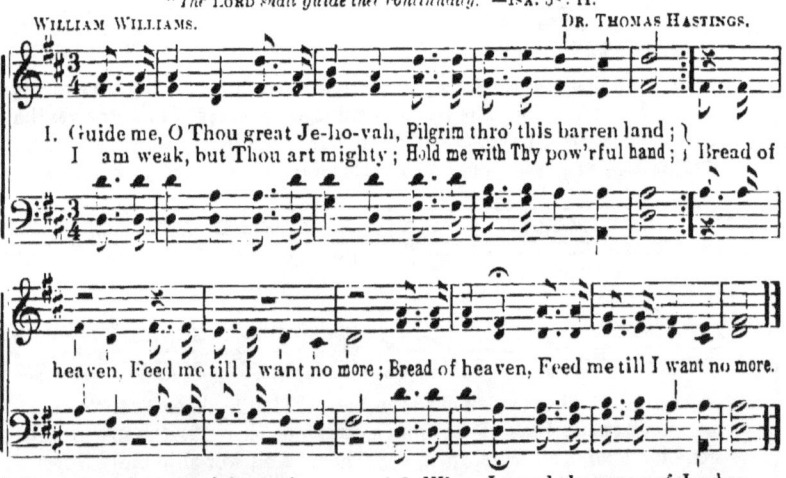

1. Guide me, O Thou great Je-ho-vah, Pilgrim thro' this barren land;
I am weak, but Thou art mighty; Hold me with Thy pow'rful hand; Bread of
heaven, Feed me till I want no more; Bread of heaven, Feed me till I want no more.

2 Open now the crystal fountain,
   Whence the healing waters flow;
Let the fiery, cloudy pillar
   Lead me all my journey through;
Strong Deliverer,
Be Thou still my strength and shield.

3 When I tread the verge of Jordan,
   Bid my anxious fears subside;
Bear me thro' the swelling current;
   Land me safe on Canaan's side;
Songs of praises
I will ever give to Thee.

231 The Lord Bless Thee.

"*The* LORD *bless thee.*" —NUM. 6 : 24.

(BENEDICTION.) W. H. DOANE.

232 The Lord Watch Between Me and Thee.

"*The* LORD *watch between me and thee.*"—GEN. 31 : 49.

(BENEDICTION.) W. H. DOANE.

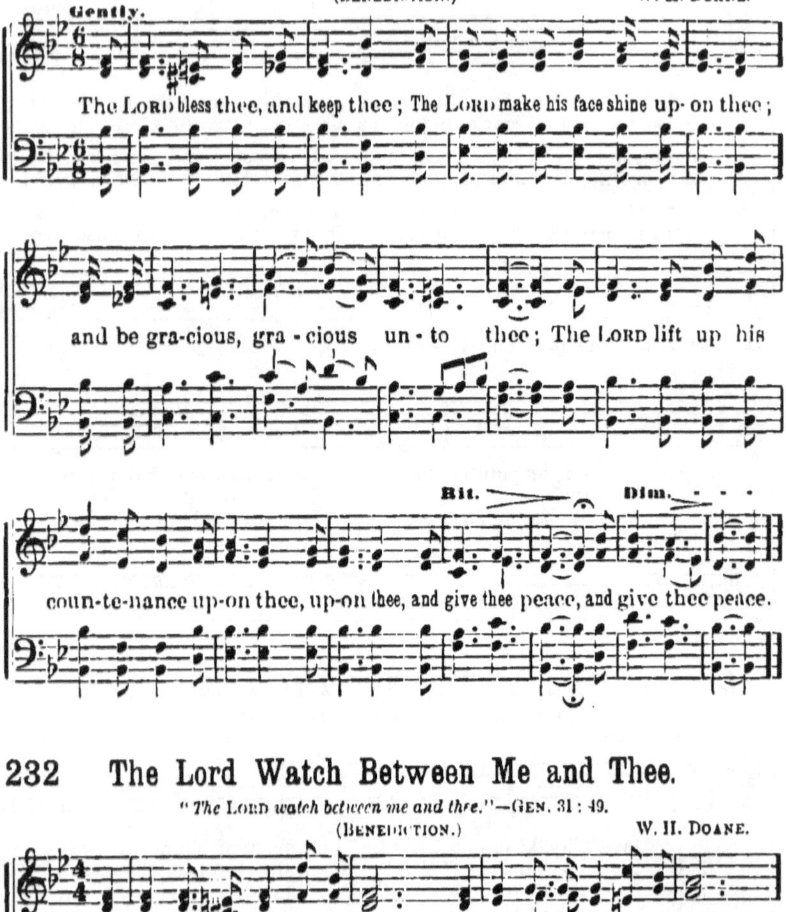

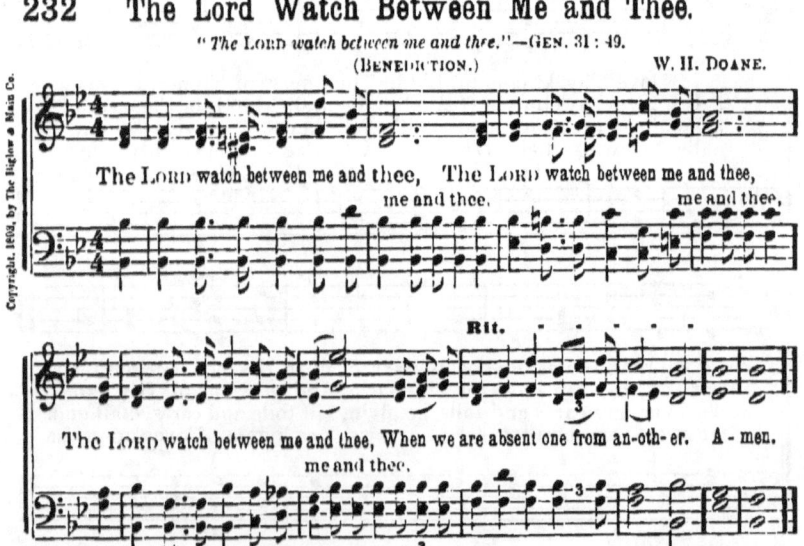

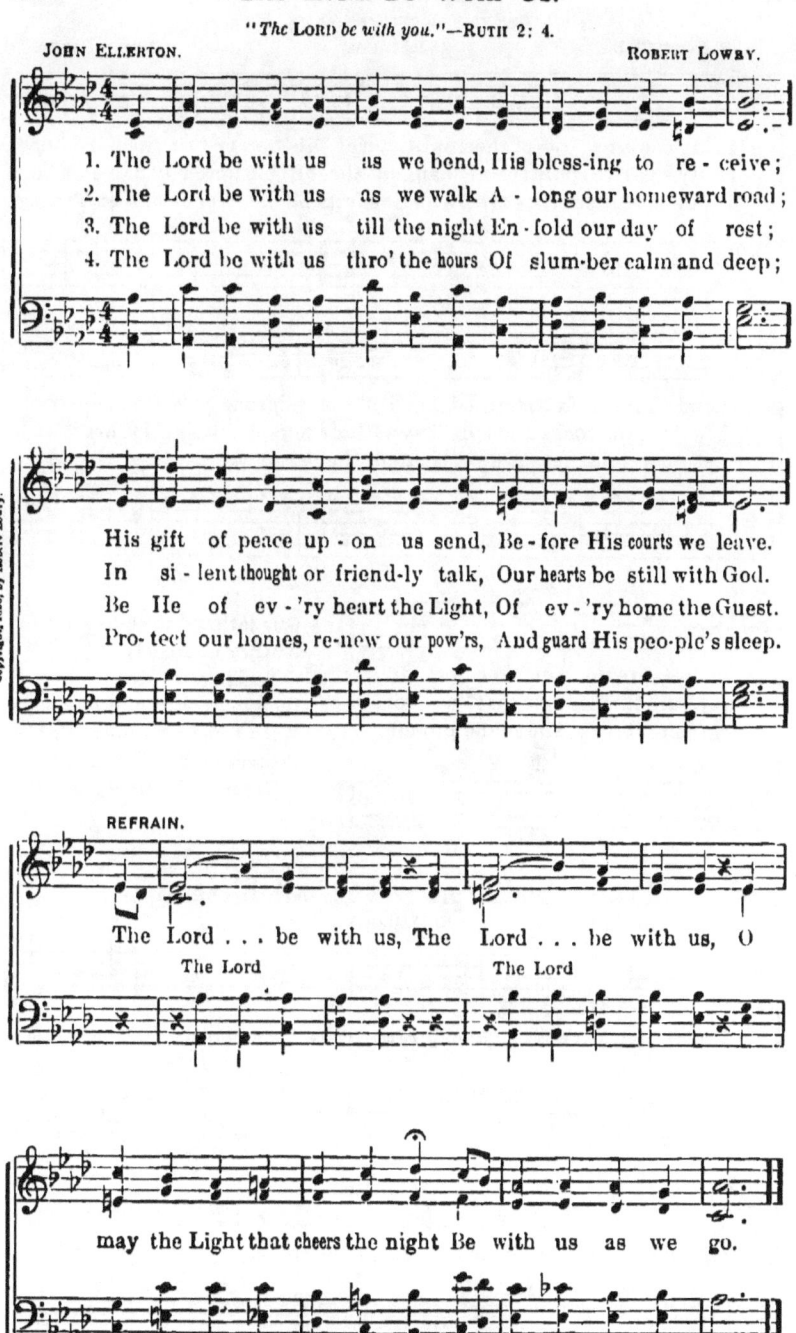

234. My Country, 'tis of Thee.

"*The glory of the country.*"—EZEK. 25: 9.

S. F. SMITH, D. D.   (AMERICA.)   HENRY CAREY.

1. My coun-try, 'tis of thee, Sweet land of lib - er- ty, Of thee I sing;
2. My na-tive country, thee, Land of the no - ble free, Thy name I love;
3. Let mu-sic swell the breeze, And ring from all the trees Sweet Freedom's song;

Land where my fa-thers died, Land of the pilgrims' pride, From ev - 'ry
I love thy rocks and rills, Thy woods and tem-pled hills; My heart with
Let mor-tal tongues a-wake, Let all that breathe par-take, Let rocks their

mountain side Let free-dom ring.
rapt-ure thrills, Like that a - bove.
si - lence break, The sound pro-long.

4 Our fathers' God, to Thee,
Author of liberty,
To Thee we sing;
Long may our land be bright
With freedom's holy light;
Protect us by Thy might,
Great God, our King.

235. Praise God, from Whom all Blessings.

REV. THOMAS KEN.   (DOXOLOGY.)   L. BOURGEOIS.

Praise God, from whom all blessings flow, Praise Him all creatures here be-low;
Praise Him a-bove, ye heav'nly host; Praise Father, Son, and Ho-ly Ghost.

TOPICAL INDEX.

ASSURANCE. No.
All the way my Saviour............ 14
Blessed assurance.................... 16
Be ye glad in the Lord.......... 97
Fade, fade each earthly joy....134
From every danger.................. 27
How firm a foundation............220
He leadeth me......................130
I am sing of my salvation..... 25
I lost my burden....................180
I know that God.....................210
My soul is rejoicing...............189
O the joy to behold................101
O happy day........................... 29
On Christ the solid rock........197
O wonderful word..................132
Salvation at Saviour's cross... 50
There's never a day...............110
What a friend we have...........227

ASPIRATION.
Dear Jesus I long.................... 8
I am Thine O Lord.................. 17
Lord, where Thou wilt........... 23
My heart shall be................... 43
More love to Thee.................. 53
My faith looks up..................135
Nearer my God......................114
Nearer my God....................... 52
O Paradise O Paradise........... 82
Take blessed Jesus................116

BIBLE.
Salvation at the Saviour's...... 50
Lamp of our feet...................149
How firm a foundation..........220

BLOOD OF CHRIST.
Alas and did........................... 22
Down at the cross.................161
From the fold........................119
In tenderness......................... 64
I gave my life........................177
Just as I am..........................183
My soul will overcome..........126
On Calvary's brow.................. 31
O could I speak.....................213
Saviour more than life..........125
There's a place for me........... 40
What can wash...................... 55

CONSECRATION.
Dear Jesus I long.................... 8
Down in the valley
I am Thine, O Lord................ 17
Inspirer and hearer................ 37
Jesus I my cross....................186
Jesus I would abide...............193
Jesus keep me......................195
Let my life be hid.................. 72
Life, labor and love................ 75
Life in His favor..................... 94
My Jesus as Thou..................102
My heart shall be................... 43
My life my love...................... 34
Must Jesus hear....................214
More like Jesus...................... 1
One more day's work............. 24
O Christ to Thee...................152
O Thou that hearest..............157
O for a closer walk................226

No.
Saviour Thy dying.................. 67
Saviour more than life..........125
Saviour keep me....................144
Take my life..........................221

COMING OF CHRIST.
I will walk............................. 28
Will Jesus find me................185

CROSS OF CHRIST.
Alas and did........................... 22
Down at the cross.................161
I lost my burden...................180
I gave my life........................177
I am coming to the cross......181
I will walk rejoicing............... 28
In the cross of Christ............133
Jesus keep me......................195
Jesus I my cross...................186
Jesus my Saviour................... 19
Must Jesus hear....................214
My trust is in........................163
On Calvary's brow.................. 31
Take the cross......................129
The cross that He.................196
Tell it again........................... 95
There's a place...................... 40
Take up thy cross................... 9

DEPENDENCE.
Guide me, O Thou.................228
Hitherto the Lord..................178
I need Thee every.................. 51
I am trusting........................179
I must tell Jesus...................184
I must have the Saviour.......123
Lord where Thou wilt............ 23
Though the night..................109

FAITH AND TRUST.
Awhile o'er the earth's......... 20
Encamped along...................115
Fairest Lord Jesus.................. 21
From every danger................. 27
He leadeth me......................130
How firm a foundation..........220
I am trusting Him.................. 74
I am trusting Thee................179
I am coming to the cross......181
Just as I am..........................183
Jesus lover of my soul........... 81
My trust is in Jesus..............163
My soul has seen..................155
My faith looks up..................135
My soul will overcome..........126
My Jesus as Thou wilt..........102
Now by faith........................170
Nearer the fount...................200
Nothing to pay...................... 68
Only trust and obey............... 79
On Christ the solid rock.......197
O Thou my soul....................209
Safe in the arms.................... 84
Salvation at the Saviour's..... 50
Take the name......................148
There's never a day...............110
Trust on, trust on................... 69
There's a promise.................. 49
We are marching...................105
Walk with the God................ 61

GIVING. No.
Give as the Lord.................... 42
Would you win......................156

GUIDANCE.
Awhile o'er earth's................ 20
All the way............................ 44
Guide me, oh Thou...............228
I must have the Saviour.......123
I cross the ever.....................131
Lord where Thou wilt............ 23
Lead, kindly Light.................. 45
Saviour Thy name.................. 30
Though the night..................109
There's never a day..............110
Take blessed Jesus................116
What shall I do..................... 32
When I walk.......................... 83

HEAVEN.
Awhile o'er earth's................ 20
Beyond the smiling...............103
Beckoning hands...................206
In exile here.........................205
Jerusalem the golden............124
Mid scenes of.......................194
Out on an ocean...................151
One sweetly solemn.............150
O the joy to behold...............104
We shall meet......................219
We are marching...................105
Where, O where..................... 73
We shall reach....................... 66

HOLY SPIRIT.
Come Thou Almighty............137
Here from the world.............120
Help me to be.......................160
Inspirer and hearer................ 37
My heart that was................108
O for a closer.......................226
There is an hour...................201

INVITATION.
Abundant pardon..................208
Do you know........................202
Hark there comes.................203
I have a Saviour...................207
Is there a heart..................... 12
Jesus is calling...................... 77
Jesus bids you......................176
Look away to Jesus..............146
Sinner choose........................ 10
There's a stranger................. 11
Though joys like.................... 59
Though your sins..................114
The King has made...............---
Today the Saviour.................164
Where................................... 73
While Jesus whispers...........182

LOYALTY.
A tribute to Thee................... 35
Encamped along...................115
Fairest Lord Jesus.................. 21
Glory, glory..........................107
Hark I hear...........................172
Hear the battle.....................122
Hear the invitation................112
In Thy name.........................141

(203)

TOPICAL INDEX.

	No.
Keep your covenant	93
Life, labor and love	75
My life, my love	34
Onward, Christian	6
O child of God	142
True hearted	154
We are soldiers	111
What shall I do	32
We are Christians	153
We have entered	167
Wherever you may	173

LOVE.

	No.
Blest be the tie	171
Drawn from a thousand	169
Glad tidings	100
I have learned	198
I love thy	230
I have a song	101
I love to tell	41
My Jesus I love	18
O love, amazing	128
To Christ our Lord	159

MISSIONARY.

	No.
Be ye glad in the Lord	97
Christian brethren	88
Drawn from a thousand	169
God bless our Gospel	204
Go ye in all the world	15
Hear the Master	145
Like the sound	191
On the wings of the morn	199
On the land	173
Preach the Gospel	65
Rescue the perishing	162
Sing His praise	192
Sowing in the morning	217
Stand up, stand up	139
There's a call	87
Throw out the life line	89
The Morning	140
Would you win	156
We have heard	48

PRAISE.

	No.
Awake, my soul	71
Awake and sing	70
All hail the power	187
Blessed assurance	16
Come, ye that love	14
Come, Thou fount	136
Come, Thou Almighty	137
From the fold	119
Glad tidings	100
Glory, Glory	107
Holy, holy, holy	38
Holy, holy, holy	36
Help me to be	160
Hark, ten thousand	229
I will sing	25
I will bless the	190
Like the sound	191
My country 'tis	234

	No.
Now to the Father	76
Only a song	5
O my heart is full	49
O give thanks	168
Onward now rejoicing	62
O could I speak	213
O praise the Lord	3
Praise God from whom	235
Rejoice with me	58
Rejoice and hail	121
Sing His praise	192
Sing a song	2
There's sunshine	4
Thou, Lord, art	188
To Christ our Lord	159
To God be the glory	99
We praise Thee	175
When morning	106
Ye saints of His	78

PRAYER.

	No.
Abide with me	224
Broken in spirit	211
Be gracious, Lord	78
Dear Jesus, I long	8
Father, whatever	158
God be with you	143
Here from the world	120
I am thine	17
Inspirer and hearer	37
I need Thee	51
Jesus, keep me	195
Jesus lover of my soul	222
Jesus, lover of my soul	81
Jesus, Saviour, Pilot	80
Lead, kindly Light	45
Let my life be	72
Life in His	184
My faith looks	135
More love to Thee	53
More like Jesus	1
Nearer My God	118
Nearer My God	52
O Thou that hearest	157
Pass me not	165
Rock of Ages	56
Say a prayer	2
Saviour, Thy name	30
Saviour, Thy	67
Saviour, breathe	86
Saviour, more	125
Saviour, keep me	144
Saviour divine	166
Sun of my soul	223
The Lord bless thee	231
The Lord watch	232
The Lord be with	233
There is an hour	201
Take, blessed Jesus	116
'Tis the blessed	57
The grace of our Lord	39

PEACE AND REST.

	No.
I am trusting	74
I lost my burden	180
My heart that was	108

	No.
Safe in the arms	84
Softly now the light	225
There comes to my heart	96

TEMPERANCE.

	No.
Jesus, Saviour	90
Throw out the life line	89
Yield not to temptation	13
We must work	216

WORSHIP

	No.
Come, ye that love	8
Glad tidings	100
Glory, glory	107
Holy, holy	138
Holy, holy	36
I have a song	101
My Jesus, I love	18
Now to the Father	76
Onward now	62
O praise the Lord	3
O worship the Lord	38
When morning	106

WARFARE.

	No.
Encamped along	115
Hark, I hear	172
Hear the battle	122
Hear the invitation	112
Jesus loves	147
Keep the banner	92
Live in the field	47
Move forward	26
Onward, Christian	6
Onward, O Christian	63
Stand up, stand up	139
Soldiers of Christ	215
We are soldiers	111
We are Christians	153

WORK.

	No.
Another day for Jesus	33
Awake, my soul	212
Go ye in all the world	15
Hear the invitation	112
Hear the Master	145
In the early	98
I have work	46
Keep the banner	92
Live on the field	47
Labor on	7
Move forward	26
One more day's work	24
Only a song	5
Onward now	62
Preach the Gospel	65
Rescue the perishing	162
Sowing in the morning	217
Stand up, stand up	139
Scatter sunshine	91
Sing a song	2
To the work	60
Take the cross	129
We must work	216
Work for the night	218

INDEX.

Titles in SMALL CAPITALS; First Lines in Roman.

	NO.		NO.
ABIDE WITH ME	224	Dear Jesus, I long to be perfectly.	8
Abundant pardon God hath said.	208	Do you know the blessed Saviour.	202
Alas, and did my Saviour bleed	22	Down at the Cross where my	161
ALL HAIL THE POWER OF JESUS	187	Down in the valley with my	80
ALL THE WAY MY SAVIOUR LEADS.	44	Drawn from a thousand	169
ALL THE WORLD IS PRAISING HIM.	191	DRAW ME NEARER	17
ANOTHER DAY FOR JESUS	33		
ANYWHERE, EVERYWHERE	65	Each cooing dove and sighing	127
AT THE CROSS	22	Encamped along the hills of light.	115
A VERY PRESENT HELP	110	ERE THE SUN GOES DOWN	46
AWAKE, AND SING	70	EVENING PRAYER	86
AWAKE, MY SOUL,	212	EVERY DAY AND HOUR	125
Awake my Soul in joyful lays	71		
Awhile o'er earth's mountains	20	Fade, fade, each earthly joy	134
A tribute to the Christ we bring	35	FATHER, WHATE'ER OF EARTHLY	158
		FAIREST LORD JESUS	21
		FAITHFUL SOLDIERS	107
BANNER OF THE CROSS	111	FAITH IS THE VICTORY	115
BEAUTIFUL BECKONING HANDS	206	FLING OUT THE BANNER	204
BEYOND THE SMILING AND THE	103	FOLLOW ON	80
BE WITH ME, LORD	131	FREELY GIVE	156
BE YE GLAD IN THE LORD	97	From every danger, doubt and	27
BLESSED ASSURANCE	16	From the fold I went astray	119
BLESSED HOUR OF PRAYER	57	FROM THE CROSS	28
BLEST BE THE TIE	171		
Broken in spirit	211	GATHERING OF THE FAITHFUL	141
BRINGING IN THE SHEAVES	217	GIVE AS THE LORD HATH	42
BY FAITH I DRAW NIGH	170	GIVE THY HEART TO ME	203
		GLAD TIDINGS	100
CALL FOR WORKERS	112	GLORY TO HIS NAME	161
CALVARY	31	Glory, glory, hallowed be His	107
CAN IT BE TRUE	95	GOD BE WITH YOU	143
CARRY THE NEWS OF JESUS	88	God bless our Gospel Workers	204
CHOOSE YE THIS DAY	10	GOD IS ABLE TO DELIVER THEE	27
Christian brethren, o'er the main.	88	Go ye in all the world	15
CHRIST, MY ROCK	25	GUIDE ME, GREAT JEHOVAH	228
CLOSE TO JESUS ALL THE WAY	109		
CLINGING TO THE HAND OF JESUS.	116	HAPPY DAY	29
COME, THOU ALMIGHTY KING	137	Hark, I hear the tramp of legions.	172
COME THOU FOUNT	136	HARK, TEN THOUSAND	229
Come, ye that love the Lord	14	Hark, there comes a whisper	203

Index.

	NO.		NO.
STILL NEAR THEE	118	To Christ, our Lord and faithful	159
SUNSHINE IN THE SOUL	4	To God Be The Glory	99
SUN OF MY SOUL	223	To The Work	60
SWEET MOMENTS OF PRAYER	120	To-Day The Saviour Calls	164
SWEET PEACE THE GIFT	96	Throw Out The Life-Line	89
		True Hearted, Whole Hearted	154
TAKE MY LIFE	221	Trust On	69
Take, blessed Jesus, my hand	116	Truth Triumphant	155
Take the cross, take the cross	129		
Take the name of Jesus with you	148	Walking In The Light	61
TAKE UP THY CROSS	9	Walk with the God of Light	61
TELL ME THE STORIES OF JESUS	85	We are Christian Soldiers pledged	153
Tell it again, let me hear the	95	We are marching to a land above	105
TELL IT TO JESUS	211	We are soldiers in the army	111
THE BIBLE	149	We have entered royal service	167
THE BOLTED DOOR	202	We have heard a joyful sound	48
THE CROSS THAT HE GAVE	196	WE PRAISE THEE, O GOD	175
THE CHRISTIAN HERO	47	WE SHALL MEET	219
THE GRACE OF OUR LORD	39	We shall reach the summer land	66
The King has made a marriage	117	We shall meet beyond the	219
THE LORD BE WITH US	233	WHAT A FRIEND	227
THE LORD BLESS THEE	231	What can wash away my stain	55
THE LORD WATCH	232	WHAT HAST THOU DONE FOR ME	177
THE MORNING LIGHT	140	WHAT SHALL I DO WITH JESUS	32
THE PORT OF PEACE	73	WHEN I WALK IN GOD'S CLEAR	83
THE PILGRIM SONG	20	When Jesus comes to reward	185
THE SAVIOUR WITH ME	123	WHEN MORNING GILDS	106
THE WEDDING GARMENT	117	WHEN THE COMFORTER CAME	108
There's a call comes ringing o'er	87	Where is my wandering boy	113
THERE'S A PLACE FOR ME	40	Where, O where is yon vessel	73
THERE'S A PROMISE FROM THE	49	WHEREVER YOU MAY BE	173
There is an hour of calm	201	WHILE HE MAY BE FOUND	208
There's a stranger at the door	11	WHILE JESUS WHISPERS	177
There's sunshine in my soul	4	WHITER THAN SNOW	8
There comes to my heart one	96	WHO WILL GO TO-DAY	145
There is never a day so dreary	110	WILL JESUS FIND US WATCHING	185
This dear old book is true	50	WORK, FOR THE NIGHT	218
'Tis the blessed hour of prayer	57	WORK TO-DAY	98
THOU, LORD, ART GOD ALONE	188	Would you win a Saviour's	156
THOUGH YOUR SINS BE AS SCARLET	114		
Though joys like the sunshine	59	Ye saints of His, sing to the Lord	78
Though the night be dark	109	YIELD NOT TO TEMPTATION	13

www.ingramcontent.com/pod-product-compliance
Lightning Source LLC
Chambersburg PA
CBHW020914230426
43666CB00008B/1457